LIBERTY TO THE CAPTIVES

CAPTIVES

TRAINING MANUAL

Praise be to the Lord,
who has not let us be torn by their teeth.

We have escaped like a bird out of the fowler's snare;
the snare has been broken, and we have escaped.

Our help is in the name of the Lord,
the maker of heaven and earth.

Psalm 124

MARK DURIE and BENJAMIN HEGEMAN

db

DEROR BOOKS

Incorporating the Fourth Edition of *Liberty to the Captives*.
Liberty to the Captives: copyright © 2022 by Mark Durie
Study Guide resources: copyright © 2022 by Benjamin Hegeman
All rights reserved.

Title: *Liberty to the Captives: Training Manual*
Description: Melbourne: Deror Books, 2022.
ISBN: 978-0-6452239-1-0

The group discussion icon is made by Freepik from www.flaticon.com.

For more information on Mark Durie's books and writings, visit markdurie.com.

For *Liberty to the Captives* resources in different languages, visit luke4-18.com.

Deror Books, Melbourne Australia
www.derorbooks.com

Contents

Foreword

Today, unprecedented numbers of former Muslims are choosing to follow Christ. Tragically, many of these find the rejection and cares of this world too much. Some national Christian leaders have even reported that 80% fall away within the first two years. What is God asking us to do about this?

In 2002 Dr Mark Durie began to teach about dhimmitude and how Christians can be free from fear of Islam and Muslims. The teaching was usually followed by a time of ministry, when people would come forward for prayer. Of those who took part in these sessions, many later testified to a powerful work of God, which brought them freedom and power for ministry.

Later Dr Durie went on to develop teaching to set people free from the spiritual bondage of Islam itself. These two teachings were combined in the book *Liberty to the Captives*.

As gospel workers around the world have got to know and use *Liberty to the Captives*, the book has been translated into many languages.

During the years since *Liberty to the Captives* was first published in 2010 it has become clear that it needed to be revised and updated, to better meet the needs of its users, particularly fellowships of Believers from a Muslim Background.

There has also been a need for a training program. At first the book's message was supported by teaching videos produced by Salaam Ministries, using PowerPoint slides. These videos were then dubbed or subtitled in other languages.

This teaching format has been used in several countries and local partners were being trained to use it. However, when Dr Benjamin Hegeman was approached by Salaam director, Nelson Wolf, about the possibility of using this approach to train bush pastors in Benin, he said, "Impossible!" and proposed a completely different approach. Drawing on decades of teaching experience in Benin, Dr Hegeman developed a training format for *Liberty to the Captives* which used a study guide. This format, which we are following here, uses small

1

discussion groups and drama, has been trialed and enthusiastically received by speakers of Baatonu, French and Hausa.

This training approach is designed to work in a wide variety of contexts, without assuming any particular educational level. Also, a leader who has completed the training should be able to take it back into their own context and train others using the same approach.

The words of Christ ring in our ears: "as the Father has sent me, so send I you" and "Go, make disciples of every people!" What did Jesus mean? The night before he died he explained that disciples know God and are united with him; they are one with God in his name, his truth, and his love (John 17). Our prayer to the Lord of the harvest is that *Liberty to the Captives* will help converts from the house of Islam stay united with God in Jesus Christ, and that it will help all those who are making disciples among Muslims.

We hope that this book—which combines Mark Durie's revised *Liberty to the Captives* teaching and Benjamin Hegeman's flexible study guides—will help meet these needs and be a blessing to the global church.

We want to express our sincere thanks to the many precious brothers and sisters who have given us feedback, making helpful suggestions to improve this resource. Your enthusiasm for this project is deeply appreciated. We also gratefully acknowledge financial supporters and the prayers of many, without whom this work could never have happened.

Mark Durie, Benjamin Hegeman, and Nelson Wolf
June 2022

How to Use This Book

Welcome to this *Liberty to the Captives Training Manual*, comprising a new edition of Mark Durie's book *Liberty to the Captives* with six core lessons and two additional lessons.

This training manual has been written for a Christian audience. It has been developed to help Christians apply the teaching in the *Liberty to the Captives* book. Our prayer is that it will help you and others to find freedom in Christ and stay free.

If you are planning to lead a training course using this training manual, please first carefully read the Guide for Leaders, which you can find before the first lesson.

We suggest that you do this training together with a group of other believers. It has been designed to be done in a conference format over 3-5 days, but it can also be done as a series of weekly small group studies.

References to the Quran use the abbreviation Q: for example, Q9:29 refers to Sura 9:29. In this training, you will learn about teachings of Islam based on authentic sources. Every effort has been made to ensure that references are to credible primary Islamic sources. Please see *The Third Choice* by Mark Durie for detailed references to many of these sources.

In making this resource available to the global church we stress that, while opposing hatred and prejudice of every kind, we believe that critical thinking should be applied to all religions and worldviews. Both Muslims and non-Muslims alike have a right to come to their own opinion about Islam, agreeing or disagreeing with its teachings as their conscience and knowledge guides them.

You can find a downloadable PDF of this training manual and other *Liberty to the Captives* resources at the website luke4-18.com. Christian ministries have permission to download, print, and share any of the resources on luke4-18.com to meet their needs.

We are always grateful to receive testimonies of how this training has helped people, as well as suggestions for improvements.

Guide for Leaders

General guidelines

This training is provided to help people find spiritual freedom from Islam.

If you are planning to lead a *Liberty to the Captives* training course, please study these guidelines carefully.

This training manual has been written to help three different types of Christians:

1. Christian converts from Islam who choose to claim their freedom in Christ

2. Christians who live, or whose ancestors have lived, alongside Muslims, under Muslim dominance

3. Anyone who would like to share the message of Christ with Muslims.

These three groups have their own distinct needs; however, we recommend that everyone (all types of Christians) does all of Lessons 1-6, which are the core lessons of this training.

There are two additional lessons, Lessons 7 and 8, which are specifically designed for Christian converts who were formerly Muslims. These should only be done after finishing the six core lessons.

- Lesson 7 discusses additional key aspects of freedom from Islam: lying, false superiority, and cursing.

- Lesson 8 provides teaching on how to grow a healthy church of people from a Muslim background. This is designed to help all who work among former Muslims.

This training has been designed to be done in a particular way. It is recommended that you follow the approach described here, as it has been tested and works well for a wide variety of learners.

This training has been designed to be completed over 3 to 5 days. It can also be followed as a series of weekly small group studies.

If you are leading training, encourage those who participate to share it with others. We expect that someone who follows this training as a participant will be able to take it back to their own context, and lead others to do the training.

The training method

This training can be followed by any number of people, from a small home group to a larger group of hundreds of people. If more than five or six people are doing the training, the participants will need to be divided into groups of around four or five. These groups stay the same and sit together throughout the training.

Ensure that all those who take part in the training have their own copy of this training manual. At the start of the training invite all participants to write their names in the front of their manuals, and let them know that their manuals are theirs to keep, and they are welcome and encouraged to make notes in them. Then explain the training manual to everyone, drawing their attention to the six core lessons, the title of each lesson, the learning objectives listed at the start of each lesson, the resources at the end of each lesson (vocabulary, names, verses from the Bible and the Quran), the questions at the end of each lesson, and the answers, which can be found at the back of the training manual.

At the beginning of each training day, each small group appoints a president and a secretary. Group members are encouraged to take turns in these roles.

- The president chairs the small group discussions and encourages everyone in the group to contribute. Only the president can consult the answers at the back of the training manual.

- The secretary takes notes on how the group answers the case study question, notes any questions to be brought to the Q&A session at the end of the lesson, and responds on behalf of the group when groups are invited by the leader to answer a question.

At the beginning of a training course, the leader instructs participants to divide into groups of four or five, explaining how the small groups will work, and that the groups need to appoint a new president and secretary each day. The leader also explains that small groups must all agree that *only the president* is allowed to look at the answers to the questions.

At the beginning of each new training day, the leader announces, "All presidents and secretaries are retired," and the small groups appoint new presidents and secretaries for the day (see below).

The training sequence for each lesson is:

- The leader announces the beginning of the lesson to all participants, inviting them to turn to the page in the training manual where the lesson starts. This page has a theme image.

- The object lesson is presented by some actors to all participants.

- The leader comments briefly on the object lesson (for just a minute or two) and draws attention to the theme image in the training manual at the start of the lesson, briefly explaining it.

- The leader reads out the learning objectives at the beginning of the lesson to all the participants. For example, "The objectives for this lesson are found on page [x]. These objectives are … [reading them all out loud]."

- Next, the case study for each lesson can be presented as a drama, but it can also be read out to everyone. If you choose to present it as a drama, the case study scenario can be rehearsed just beforehand: encourage the participants to act these scenarios out. After this drama (or reading) the small groups meet to discuss the case study and answer the question at the end of it: "How will you respond?" After this, the secretary of each group reports back to the larger group on how their group answered the question.

- Each lesson needs to be broken down into a series of sessions, except for the first lesson, which is short, and can be done in a single session.

- For each session within a lesson, participants follow steps 1 to 5 below:

  1. The leader announces which sections will be discussed in this session, together with the page numbers in the training manual. (The leader may wish to follow the division markers provided in the text which suggest how much to cover in each small group session.)

  2. Someone with a good reading voice reads the text aloud for the sections to be discussed. (If the training is following the division markers, the reader will read to the marker, which will take about 10-15 minutes.)

  3. Participants break up into small groups and are directed to the questions for the current session. The questions can be found at the end of each lesson.

  4. The groups discuss and answer the questions for the sections in the current session. This could take about 10-20 minutes, depending on the number of questions. During this time the leader moves around from group to group to keep an eye on how they are going.

  5. When the leader observes that one of the groups has finished for that session, all the other groups are asked to finish up. Keep moving with the material; do not wait for stragglers.

     Repeat steps 1 to 5 for the remaining sessions until the whole lesson has been completed.

- At the end of each lesson, all the groups come back together for a question-and-answer session on that lesson.

Lessons 5, 6 and 7 end with prayers. Please follow the advice given below for administering the prayers.

This is the discussion icon, showing three people talking:

This icon indicates a suggested pause point for group sessions. This is just a suggestion: each leader needs to plan how to divide the lessons for their training, depending on the needs of their participants. The amount of information that participants can absorb at one time will vary depending on the group, so the training leader will need to decide how much material is appropriate to cover in each small group session.

Object lessons

It is recommended that you introduce each lesson with an object lesson, enacted in a drama. If you choose to use it, there is also an object lesson for introducing the whole training. You will need to prepare for the object lessons in advance. In many cases it will be enough if the actors meet to rehearse the object lesson half an hour beforehand.

Object lesson to introduce the whole training

Find six to eight chairs strong enough to hold the weight of a person standing on the chair. Place the chairs in line, the front of each chair up against the back of the next chair. Next ask a young participant to walk on the chairs while pretending to talk on his mobile phone. Then make it harder, separating the chairs more and more until it becomes quite difficult. Then finally have someone hold up a piece of paper saying "GUIDE". This person then goes and holds the participant's hand as he steps from chair to chair, illustrating how the guiding hand makes it so much easier to perform what is hard to do by yourself.

Object lesson for Lesson 1

A man is walking along shouting, "I am free! I am free!" and talking loudly about how free he is as a Christian. But all the time he is ignoring two goats tied to his legs, one goat to one leg and the other goat to the other leg. (Another animal could also work, such as two sheep, two roosters, or two cats.) It is hard for him to walk in a straight line. He is being pulled first one way and then the other. He struggles to reach his destination but he just cannot see the goats. He thinks he is free, but he is not. Not at all!

If animals are not available, get a large poster-sized sheet of paper and have someone draw a person or a couple with two goats tied to their legs. Have someone come up, point to the drawing and say, "I am this Believer from a Muslim Background! I am free, I am free." He or she talks about his/her freedom for one minute yet completely ignores the goats and does not mention them. This person exits, then another person comes in, uses a pointer to point to the goats, and then raises his hands in a questioning way.

Object lesson for Lesson 2

Have the word "DHIMMI" printed in bold letters with a thick-tipped marker on a wide piece of masking tape. Show the audience the word on the tape, and then go and tape it over the mouth of a person who is already tied to a chair. Then, after 20 seconds, have the person look up and try to stand up. He or she can't. Have another adult hold up a paper on which is written in bold "REDEEMER". Have the redeemer untie the *dhimmi* and then have the liberated *dhimmi* walk to a shining light (this could be a lamp, or even the torch on a smartphone), reciting Psalm 23 out loud from memory.

Object lesson for Lesson 3

If an animal takes the bait of a trap, it is caught. It cannot get free until it lets go of the bait. Find a jar just big enough for someone to put their hand in it, but small enough that if they make a fist they cannot get their hand out. Hold up the jar and a sheet of paper saying "SHAHADA". Put some nuts inside. The person puts their hand in to grab the nuts, but cannot get their hand out. They walk around showing everyone their problem. The only way they can get their hand free is to let go of the nuts.

Object lesson for Lesson 4

An agitated veiled woman and a Muslim man with a prayer hat sit blindfolded on two chairs. Have the words "DEVOUT MUSLIM" in big letters written on two sheets of paper and then taped to each person's chest or hung around their necks. Have several people come in and walk around them several times making joyful loud whispering noises to each other, and singing a praise song tune together, but saying nothing directly to the Muslims. Have the Muslim man reach for a sword (or some other weapon such as a machete) under his chair each time someone comes near and wave it in the air, telling them to be quiet and not to provoke him to violence. The others quietly exit. Someone then comes and quietly removes the blindfolds and shows the couple that there is no one there. Then all exit looking very surprised.

Object lesson for Lesson 5

A man or woman is lying on the ground, looking exhausted and defeated, curled up in a defensive posture. The word "REJECTED" is printed in bold print on a piece of paper and taped to the person. A long rope around one ankle leads off, away from the scene. You cannot see what it is tied to: it could be tied to a tree or something else. A redeemer figure comes, undoes the rope, gently lifts or guides the person up onto a chair, gives them a glass of water, watches patiently until they have finished drinking, then takes the glass, puts it to one side, and takes off the label "REJECTED". Then the redeemer figure kneels down in front of the redeemed person on the chair and washes and dries their feet.

Object lesson for Lesson 6

Have a man sit on a chair behind a desk holding his Bible with his wife standing behind him with her hands on his shoulders. They look at the open Bible in silence. Have the word "DHIMMI" printed in bold letters with thick-tipped marker on a wide piece of masking tape. Show the audience the word on the tape, and then go and tape it over the mouth of the man on the chair. Then have a pretend Muslim walk in and begin to greet and then mock the silent, seated Christian. Have the wife attempt to answer the questions. The Muslim ignores her answers. Have the Christian continue to hold the Bible with two hands but only nod and move his head. Finally, have the Muslim laugh and leave. Have the wife remove the tape over the husband's mouth and have him say with joy, "Tell the Muslim to come back!" She quickly leaves in the direction of the Muslim. Then the man decides to follow her, saying, "I am coming, I am coming!" holding up the Bible as he does.

Object lesson for Lesson 7

Quietly place three chairs before the audience, a single chair on one side, and a pair of chairs next to each other on the other side. Each of the paired chairs has the word "FREEDOM" attached to it on a sheet of paper. The other chair has the word "ISLAM" attached to it. This single chair is tied by a rope to something immovable in the room. A person is sitting in the "Islam" chair, his leg tied by another shorter rope to that chair. The rope is not long enough to allow him to reach the "freedom" chairs, and the "Islam" chair cannot be moved because it is tied to something immovable. Have the word "BONDAGE" printed in bold letters with a thick-tipped marker on a sheet of paper. Someone shows this sheet of paper to the audience and then goes and tapes it to the rope holding the person to the "Islam" chair. Have someone else enter and sit in one of the "freedom" chairs, reading a Bible. This person beckons to the bound person, inviting them to come over to the vacant "freedom" chair. The bound person tries to reach the "freedom" chair, but cannot because of the ropes. The person in the "freedom" chair takes up a sign with "RENOUNCE" printed on it and shows it to the audience. That person then goes over and attaches the "RENOUNCE" sign above the "ISLAM" sign so both are visible, and unties the rope that binds the person to the "Islam" chair. Both people now go over and sit down in the two "freedom" chairs. They start singing the first verse of 'Amazing Grace' (or some other well-known hymn or song about freedom in Christ) together.

Object lesson for Lesson 8

Have a woman dressed like a devout Muslim come in blindfolded, led to a chair by the hand of a man who looks like a Muslim. The word "SHAME" is printed on a sheet of paper and taped to her chest. The Muslim man says to her, "Your feet and hands are filthy!" and walks away. She is seated on the chair, and the audience can see that she has very dirty feet and dirty hands. She is weeping softly. In comes a Christian woman. She carries a basin with water in it, and a towel. She first gently and quietly wipes away the tears and dries the woman's cheeks. Then she washes the woman's hands, and then kneels to wash her feet. After the feet are cleansed, the Christian woman then gently removes the veil and helps the other woman up. They walk away hand in hand, the Christian carrying the basin and the Muslim carrying the towel.

The role of small group presidents

A small group president's role is to encourage discussion in their group.

When a word is in bold print in the questions for each lesson, this means that it is in the new names or new vocabulary for that particular lesson. When a group comes across one of these words, the president may wish to take a moment to draw the group's attention to who the person was, or what the meaning of the word is.

The president encourages everyone in their group to contribute to the discussion.

The questions provided are to help make sure everyone has understood the teaching. It is good if members of the group also want to discuss the issues in the section further.

If a group goes off-topic, the president can bring them back to the questions being studied.

The president also makes sure the discussion keeps moving along.

The small group president is the only person in the small group who is allowed to consult the answers at the end of the training manual.

Administering the prayers in Lessons 5-7

Here are guidelines for administering the prayers renouncing the *shahada,* the *dhimma,* and lying, false superiority, and cursing in Lessons 5-7.

- Say the prayers all together as a large group (not separately, in the small groups). However, participants do not need to move out of their groups unless that is necessary to gather everyone together.

- It is best if everyone is invited to stand while saying the prayers: we should be alert, awake, and standing when making such declarations.

- Before each prayer session, Bible verses are set out in question-and-answer format. The leader first reads the questions, then the scripture verses, then the answers (printed in italics). After this everyone stands and says the prayer together. When Lesson 6 (Freedom from the *Dhimma*) is done following Lesson 5 (Freedom from the *Shahada*)—this is the usual order—then the 'truth encounter' verses have already been read out for Lesson 5 so they do not need to be repeated for Lesson 6.

- In Lesson 5, the prayer renouncing the *shahada* should be said just after the 'Declaration and Prayer of Commitment to Follow Jesus Christ', also found in Lesson 5. Recite the 'Declaration and Prayer of Commitment to Follow Jesus Christ' together first and then read the testimonies of freedom. After this the leader reads out the 'truth encounter' verses. Then everyone says the 'Declaration and Prayer to Renounce the *Shahada* and Break Its Power' together.

- These prayers can be said together in a few different ways:

  - People can read them together directly from this training manual.

  - If projection is used, they can read them from a screen.

  - Often it will be best to read them in a 'repeat-after-me' format, in which the leader calls out a phrase, and others repeat the phrase. The repeat-after-me format is good when participants are not used to reading text out loud together. This method also gives people more time to process and own the words of the prayers for themselves; this format can build a sense of unity for a group.

- Every time these prayers are recited, it is very important, immediately after people say the prayers, for the leader to pray over all those who have recited the prayers to break curses and replace them with blessings. These follow-up prayers by the leader should include the following elements:

  - The leader should confidently declare a breaking of all curses associated with what has been renounced. This can either be done for the people, or the leader can lead the people in making the declaration for themselves. For example, after the prayer renouncing the *shahada*, the leader could say, "I break from your life all curses brought by Islam. I break from your life all the spiritual powers of

14

Islam." Or if the people are being led, they could use the words, in repeat-after-me format, "I break from my life all curses brought by Islam. I break from my life all the spiritual powers of Islam."

- Likewise, the leader commands demons to leave—casting them out—or leads the people in doing this for themselves, using these words: "In the name of our Lord Jesus Christ I command all demons to submit to Jesus and leave you now" (or "leave me now" if using a repeat-after-me format).

- The leader then blesses the people who have recited the prayers, invoking blessings that impart the opposite of what has been renounced, as explained in Lesson 2. For example, after the prayer to renounce the *dhimma*, the leader can bless the lips of the people with words of life to speak the truth boldly; and after the prayer to renounce the *shahada*, the leader can bless the people with life, hope, courage, and the love of God.

- In addition, it is good to have a prayer team ready who can continue to pray for people after a prayer has been recited together. One way is to have an anointing ministry line: after reciting the prayer, the people can be invited to come forward to be anointed with oil, and prayed for individually by the prayer team members. It is good to train your prayer team in advance, so they know what is expected of them.

Baptism

It is strongly recommended that some time before their baptism every person who has left Islam to follow Christ should formally recite both of the prayers in Lesson 5: the 'Declaration and Prayer of Commitment to Follow Jesus Christ' and the 'Declaration and Prayer to Renounce the *Shahada* and Break Its Power'. Before they recite these prayers the meaning of the prayers should be explained clearly to them, so they can understand and be fully committed to what they are praying. It is recommended that this be done as part of the preparation for baptism.

Manifestations

It sometimes happens when people say these prayers that demons will manifest. Someone might start crying out, they might fall over, or they might start shaking. For this reason, and especially when people recite the prayers in a group, it is good to be prepared. Have a team or teams on hand who can carefully take a person aside, encourage them, and gently but confidently command the demon(s) to leave. It is also good to have one or more leaders with their eyes open and looking around during the prayers to keep watch on how everyone is doing.

1

The Need to Renounce Islam

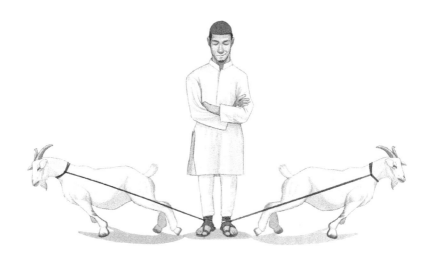

"For freedom Christ has set us free!"
Galatians 5:1

Lesson objectives

a. Grasp the critical need to renounce the covenantal powers in Islam.

b. Understand the aggression of Islam's spiritual sovereignty over Muslims and non-Muslims.

c. Be introduced to the idea of being transferred from Satan's power into the kingdom of Jesus Christ.

d. Dismiss the use of force as the final answer to Islamic *jihad*.

e. Consider the resemblance of Muhammad to the "fierce king" seen by Daniel in a vision, and understand that this king was defeated, but "not by human power."

Case study: What would you do?

As you are reading through this book by Mark Durie, you receive a call informing you that your uncle was in a small car accident and that he is in a hospital very near you. When you go to visit him, you find out he is sharing a room with Ali, a very devout Shiite Muslim. After you pray for your uncle, Ali is eager to talk to you, and says, "You would become a very good Muslim and you are very close to doing so. Once you learn about the wonderful example of Hazrat Muhammad, peace be upon him, you will see that he was promised and prophesied to come by Hazrat Isa, peace be upon him. Our Great Prophet, peace be upon him, was the most merciful, the most loving, the most peaceful person ever to live on earth. I invite you to enter the true path of Allah."

How will you reply? What will you do?

An urgent need

This is the testimony of a former Muslim who embraced the Christian faith and then later expressed great freedom when he renounced Islam:

> I was raised in a Muslim family in the West. We did attend mosque and learned to say our prayers in Arabic. Beyond that, I was not too religious growing up. Things changed when I went through a period of searching as I went off to university. At the end of this period, I discovered who Jesus Christ really was, and he saved my soul.
>
> I got involved with a student Christian group at the university campus. Every week, a different student took turns sharing a message from the Bible. I had been a Christian less than a year, but they asked me if I might share a message nevertheless. The evening I was supposed to share, I stepped into one of the campus libraries for some prayer. The message I was to speak about was "Jesus died for me; would I die for Jesus?"
>
> As I began to pray, something very strange happened. I felt a tightening in my throat as if I was being strangled or suffocated. Panic came upon me as this sensation continued and intensified. Then I felt a voice telling me, "Renounce Islam! Renounce Islam!" I believed it was the Lord. At the same time, my mind rationalized: "Lord, I haven't really been 'into' Islam or practicing at all lately."
>
> However, the sense of suffocation continued, so I said, "In the name of Jesus, I renounce Islam." All of this was happening somewhat quietly, since it was a library. Immediately, the sense of pressure around my throat was released. A feeling of great relief came over me! I went back to prayer and preparation for the meeting. At the meeting the Lord really showed up in power and I remember students on their knees and faces crying out to the Lord and offering themselves to him.

One of the urgent needs of many people in the world today is to renounce Islam. This book explains why this is necessary and how to do it. It provides information and prayers to help Christians become free from the controlling spiritual influence of Islam.

The key idea of this book is that Islam's spiritual power is exercised through two covenants (or pacts), known as the *shahada* and the *dhimma*. The *shahada* binds Muslims and the *dhimma* binds non-Muslims to conditions determined by Islamic law.

It is important to know:

- how a person who was a Muslim but has chosen to follow Christ can renounce and be set free from covenantal allegiance to the *shahada* and all that it entails.

- how a Christian can claim their freedom and be released from the demeaning inferiority forced on non-Muslims by Islamic *sharia* law through the *dhimma*.

Christians can claim their rightful freedom from both of these covenants by renouncing them. (For this purpose, prayers for renouncing Islam are provided later in this book.)

The two covenants

The Arabic word *Islam* means 'submission' or 'surrender'. The faith of Muhammad makes two kinds of submission available to the world. One is the surrender of the convert who accepts the religion of Islam. The other is the surrender of the non-Muslim who submits to Islamic dominance without conversion.

The covenant of the convert is the *shahada*, the Muslim creed. This is a confession of faith in the unity of Allah and the prophethood of Muhammad, and all that these entail.

The covenant of the non-Muslim who surrenders to Islamic political dominance is the *dhimma*. This is an institution of Islamic law which determines the status of Christians and others who choose not to convert to Islam but are compelled to live under its rule.

Islam's demand that humankind submit, either by confessing the *shahada,* or by accepting the *dhimma*, must be resisted.

Many Christians would understand that someone who has left the Muslim faith to follow Christ might need to renounce Islam. However, many Christians may be surprised to learn that Christians who have never been Muslims can nevertheless come under the spiritual influence of Islamic dominance. To resist this, they need to take a personal stand against the claims of the *dhimma* covenant, rejecting the fear and inferiority that Islam seeks to impose upon them as non-Muslims.

We will explore the principles behind these twin covenants of dominance—the *shahada* and the *dhimma*—and invite you to consider Christ, the power of his life, and the spiritual resources for freedom that he has secured through the cross. Biblical principles are given and prayers provided that enable you to claim for yourself the freedom that Christ has already secured on your behalf.

Transfer of sovereignty

Many Islamic teachers emphasize that sovereignty is "only for Allah." When they say this they mean that *sharia* law must rule over other principles of justice or power.

A key idea of this book is that followers of Christ have a right and indeed a duty to renounce other forms of spiritual sovereignty.

In a Christian understanding, turning to Christ means rejecting and renouncing all spiritual claims over one's soul except those of Christ. Paul, in his letter to the Colossians, described coming to faith in Christ as being transferred from one kingdom to another:

> For he has rescued us from the dominion of darkness and brought us into the kingdom of the Son he loves, in whom we have redemption, the forgiveness of sins. (Colossians 1:13-14)

The spiritual strategy proposed in this book is an application of this principle of being transferred from one kingdom to another. The Christian believer, through their redemption, has come under Christ's rule. As such they are no longer subject to the principles of the "dominion of darkness."

For believers to claim and own this freedom for themselves—which is their birthright—in opposition to Islam's claims, they need to understand what they have been transferred *from*, and what they have been transferred *into*. This book offers this knowledge and provides resources to apply it.

The sword is not the answer

There are many ways to resist Islam's will to dominate. This can involve a wide range of actions, including political and community action, human rights advocacy, academic inquiry, and the use of media to communicate the truth. For some communities and nations there are times when a military response may be necessary, but the sword cannot be the final answer to Islamic *jihad*.

When Muhammad commissioned his followers to take his faith to the world, he instructed them to offer *three* choices to non-Muslims. One was conversion (the *shahada*), another was political surrender (the *dhimma*), and another choice was the sword: to fight for their lives, killing and being killed, as the Quran teaches (Q9:111; see also Q2:190-193, 216-217; Q9:5, 29).

The path of military resistance to *jihad* brings spiritual dangers, quite apart from the possibility of being defeated. When the Christians of Europe embarked on defensive resistance to Islamic conquest they had to take up the sword for more than a thousand years. The *Reconquista* to liberate the Iberian Peninsula took almost 800 years. Only seven years after Arabs sacked Rome in 846 AD, and more than a century after the Muslim invasion and occupation of Andalusia (the Iberian Peninsula), Pope Leo IV in 853 AD promised paradise to those who gave their lives defending Christian churches and cities against the *jihad*. However, this was an attempt to fight Islam by copying its tactics: after all, it was Muhammad, not Jesus, who had promised paradise to those who die in battle.

Yet the root of the power of Islam is not military or political, but spiritual. In its conquests, Islam made what are in essence *spiritual* demands, expressed in *sharia* law through the institutions of the *shahada* and the *dhimma*, and backed by military force. For this reason the resources offered here to resist and liberate people from Islam are spiritual. They are designed to be put to use by Christian believers, as they apply a biblical understanding of the cross to provide a pathway for people to come into freedom.

"Not by human power"

In the Book of Daniel there is a striking prophetic vision, given six centuries before Christ, of a ruler whose reign would arise out of the kingdoms that came after the empire of Alexander the Great:

> In the latter part of their reign, when rebels have become completely wicked, a fierce-looking king, a master of intrigue, will arise. He will become very strong, but not by his own power. He will cause astounding devastation and will succeed in whatever he does. He will destroy those who are mighty, the holy people. He will cause deceit to prosper, and he will consider himself superior. When they feel secure, he will destroy many and take his stand against the prince of princes. Yet he will be destroyed, but not by human power. (Daniel 8:23-25)

The characteristics and impact of this ruler bear a remarkable resemblance to Muhammad and his legacy, including Islam's sense of superiority; its hunger for success; the use of deception; seizing the strength and riches of others and using them to gain power; again and again defeating nations who had a false sense of security; opposition to Jesus, Son of God and the crucified Lord of all; and a track record of devastating Christian and Jewish communities.

Could this prophecy refer to Muhammad and the religion of Islam, which arose from the moral and spiritual wreckage of Muhammad's life and legacy, as reported by Muslim sources? This legacy is clear. If it does refer to Muhammad, then Daniel's prophecy offers hope of eventual victory over the power of this "king," but it also contains a warning that victory will not be by "human power." To overcome this "fierce-looking king," liberty will not and cannot be won through means that are merely political, military, or economic.

This warning certainly holds true for Islam's claimed right to dominate others. The power behind this claim is spiritual, and effective resistance leading to lasting freedom can only be achieved by spiritual means. Other forms of resistance, including military force, may be necessary to manage the symptoms of Islam's will to dominate, but they cannot address the root of the problem.

Only the power of Christ and his cross provide the keys to lasting and final release from Islam's demeaning claims. It is out of that conviction that this book has been written. Its purpose is to equip believers to find freedom from the two aspects of Islam's strategy to dominate the human soul.

Study Guide

Lesson 1

Vocabulary

covenant   *sharia*   Iberian Peninsula
shahada   *jihad*   Andalusia
dhimma   *Reconquista*

New names

- Roman Pope Leo IV (in office from 847–855 AD)
- Alexander the Great (356–323 BC)

Bible in this lesson

Colossians 1:13-14   Daniel 8:23-25

Quran in this lesson

Q2:190, 193, 217   Q9:29, 111

Questions Lesson 1

- Small group members introduce themselves and appoint a group president and secretary.
- Discuss the case study.

An urgent need

1. What did the Holy Spirit tell the former Muslim to do before presenting his message to Christians?

2. What does Durie see as one of the most urgent needs of many people?

3. What are the Arabic names for the two spiritual **covenants** in Islam?

4. Which type of person needs to be set free and renounce the **shahada**?

5. Which type of person needs to be released from the demeaning inferiority imposed by Islamic **sharia** law?

The two covenants

6. What two forms of surrender are required by the faith of Muhammad?

7. What does reciting the **shahada** imply?

8. What is the **dhimma** covenant?

9. What might surprise many Christians about the spiritual influence of Islamic dominance?

Transfer of sovereignty

10. What do Muslim teachers mean when they say that "sovereignty is only for Allah"?

11. What must every Christian renounce and reject when they turn to Christ?

12. From what have Christians been transferred? Into what are they transferred?

The sword is not the answer

13. To resist Islam, what are the actions which Durie suggests Christians may possibly take?

14. What were the three choices that Muhammad instructed his followers to offer conquered non-Muslims?

15. How long were Christians fighting Islamic forces after Christian lands were invaded, and how long did the Christian pushback—called the *Reconquista*—take to win back the **Iberian Peninsula**?

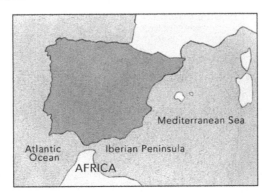

16. After Muslims sacked Rome in 846 AD, what did **Pope Leo IV** promise Christian soldiers in 853 AD if they fought back against Arab invaders?

17. According to Durie, what is the root of the power of Islam?

"Not by human power"

18. To whom, according to Durie, does Muhammad's legacy bear a remarkable resemblance?

19. Note the various aspects of Islam that cause it to resemble the ruthless king in the Book of Daniel (complete each phrase):

- Islam's sense of …

- Islam's hunger for …

- Islam's use of …

- Islam taking and using strength and riches …

- Islam defeating nations …
- Islam's opposition to …
- Islam's track record of …

20. How will victory eventually come?

21. What two keys alone can offer release from Islam's demeaning claims?

2

Freedom through the Cross

"He has sent me to proclaim freedom for the captives."
Luke 4:18

Lesson objectives

a. Understand that Jesus promised to set people free.

b. Understand that we can choose to claim our freedom.

c. Identify titles of Satan used in the Bible, and understand what they mean.

d. Understand that Satan's power has been broken through the cross and that we have been transferred out of his control.

e. Recognize that we are engaged in a struggle against evil powers.

f. Identify six strategies that Satan uses to accuse us and how we can be alert to these strategies.

g. Recognize how Satan uses open doors and footholds in human lives.

h. Identify strategies for closing doors and removing footholds that Satan uses against us.

i. Understand the spiritual authority given by Jesus Christ to his disciples, and know how to apply this authority to set people free.

j. Understand the 'principle of specificity' and why it is important for claiming our freedom.

k. Consider five steps for helping people to be set free.

Case study: What would you do?

You are a church youth worker and you have been invited to a national youth conference which includes a number of prominent Believers from a Muslim Background. You are being housed in a nice school dorm with four beds per room. Two of your roommates, Hassan and Hussein, are twins who are Christian brothers from a Muslim background. Before going to bed, Patrick, another older youth leader, invites you and the other two men to join him for prayer. You all gladly accept, and Patrick prays for spiritual protection during the night. At around 4 am, Hassan begins shouting and seems very spiritually agitated. Patrick, Hussein, and you gather around Hassan to pray for him. As Patrick prays, Hassan becomes even more terrified.

Patrick says to Hussein, "Since you came out of Islam, have you renounced the covenants, vows or agreements of your past?"

Hussein seems shocked and says, "That's crazy. We never did anything like that in Islam. We just went to the mosque, man, and now we're Christians. My brother Hassan is only struggling with anxiety like any other folks do. This has nothing to do with religion." Then Hussein looks at you and says, "Do you believe we should have renounced something? Do you believe there is some kind of demon in our background, or something?"

What will you say?

———

Reza was a young man who had decided to leave Islam and follow Jesus Christ. At a meeting one evening he was invited to say a prayer rejecting Islam. He very willingly started to do this. However, during the prayer, when he came to say the words, "I renounce the example of Muhammad," he found to his great surprise that he could not say the word 'Muhammad'. This shocked him, because although he grew up in a Muslim family, he had never liked Islam and had not practiced it for a long time. His Christian friends gathered around him and encouraged him with words that reminded him of his authority in Jesus Christ. After this he was able to complete the prayer, saying the words that renounced the example of Muhammad.

Two things changed in Reza's life after that night. First, he was healed of a life-long habit of getting very angry at others; and second, he became effective in evangelism and discipling others who had left Islam. That night, when Reza renounced Islam he received an anointing of power for evangelism and discipleship, which was a key to his effectiveness in ministry. He was set free to serve the gospel.

This chapter is about how to be set free from the power of Satan. This prepares the way for the chapters to follow, which focus on Islamic bondages.

The principles taught in this chapter can be applied in many different situations, not just to do with Islam.

Jesus starts to teach

In his letter to the Romans, Paul spoke about "the glorious freedom of the children of God" (Romans 8:21). This "glorious freedom" is the birthright of every Christian. It is a great gift, a precious inheritance that God wants to give to everyone who trusts and follows Jesus.

When Jesus began his ministry of teaching, his very first public teaching was about freedom. This took place just after Jesus' baptism by John the Baptist, and after he was tempted by Satan in the desert. When Jesus came back from the desert, he immediately started preaching the gospel. How did he do this? He did it by introducing himself. We read in Luke that Jesus stood up in the synagogue at Nazareth, his home village, and began to read from the Book of Isaiah, chapter 61:

> "The Spirit of the Lord is on me,
> because he has anointed me
> to proclaim good news to the poor.
> He has sent me to proclaim freedom for the prisoners
> and recovery of sight for the blind,
> to set the oppressed free,
> to proclaim the year of the Lord's favor."

> Then he rolled up the scroll, gave it back to the attendant and sat down. The eyes of everyone in the synagogue were fastened on him. He began by saying to them, "Today this scripture is fulfilled in your hearing." (Luke 4:18-21)

Jesus was telling the people that he came to set people free. He was saying that the promise of freedom, given to Isaiah, was being fulfilled "today": the people of Nazareth were meeting with the One who can bring freedom to captives. He was also telling them that he was anointed by the Holy Spirit: he was the Anointed One, the Messiah, God's chosen King, their promised Savior.

Jesus was inviting them to choose freedom. He was bringing good news: hope for the poor, release for captives in prison, healing for the blind, and freedom for all who are oppressed.

Everywhere Jesus went he brought freedom to people—real freedom, in many different ways. When we read the Gospels, we hear about Jesus doing good for many people: giving hope to the hopeless, feeding the hungry, setting people free from the power of demons, and healing the sick.

Jesus is still bringing people freedom today. Every Christian is called by Jesus to enjoy the freedom that he brings.

When Jesus announced in the synagogue that he was proclaiming the "year of the Lord's favor," he was telling the people that this was their special time for God to show them his favor. Jesus was telling them that God was coming with power and love to set people free and they could be set free too.

Will you hope and believe that reading this book can be your special time for you to experience God's grace and freedom?

A time to choose

Imagine you are trapped in a cage, and the door to the cage is locked. Every day food and water are brought to you in the cage. You can live there, but you are a prisoner. Suppose someone comes along and unlocks the door to that cage. Now you have a choice. You can keep on living in the cage, or you can step out of it and discover what life is like outside the cage. It is not enough for the door to the cage to be open. You have to choose to step out of that cage. If you do not choose to be free, it is just as if you are still locked in.

When Paul wrote to the Galatians, he said, "For freedom Christ has set us free. Stand firm, therefore, and do not submit again to a yoke of slavery." (Galatians 5:1) Jesus Christ came to set people free, and once we know the freedom he brings, we have a choice to make. Will we choose to live as free people?

Paul is saying that we need to be awake and alert to claim our freedom. To live in freedom, we must understand what it means to be free, then claim our own freedom, and then walk in it. When we are following Jesus we need to learn how to "stand firm" and reject the "yoke of slavery."

This teaching is designed to help everyone choose to be free and then to live as free people.

In the next few sections we learn about Satan's role, how we are transferred from Satan's power into the Kingdom of God, and the spiritual battle that we are engaged in.

Satan and his kingdom

The Bible says that we have an enemy, someone who wants to destroy us. He is called Satan. He has many helpers. Some of these helpers are called demons.

Jesus describes Satan's way with people in John 10:10, calling Satan "the thief": "The thief comes only to steal and kill and destroy. I came that they may have life, and have it abundantly." What a powerful contrast! Jesus brings life—abundant life; Satan brings loss, destruction, and death. Jesus also tells us that Satan "was a murderer from the beginning" (John 8:44).

According to the Gospels and the letters of the New Testament, Satan has a genuine but limited power and sovereignty over this world. His kingdom is called the "dominion of darkness" (Colossians 1:13) and he is called:

- "the prince of this world" (John 12:31)
- "the god of this age" (2 Corinthians 4:4)
- "the ruler of the kingdom of the air" (Ephesians 2:2)
- "the spirit who is now at work in those who are disobedient" (Ephesians 2:2).

The apostle John even teaches us that the whole world is under the control of Satan: "We know that we are children of God, and that the whole world is under the control of the evil one." (1 John 5:19)

If we understand that the "whole world is under the control of the evil one," we should not be surprised to see evidence of Satan's work in all the cultures, ideologies, and religions of this world. Satan is even active in the church.

For this reason, we also need to consider the possible imprint of evil in Islam, its worldview, and its spiritual power; but first we will consider general principles of how to be set free from evil.

The great transfer

J. L. Houlden, Fellow of Trinity College Oxford, wrote an overview of Paul's theological worldview. Paul, he says:

> ... had convictions about man. Not only is man sinfully and willfully alienated from God ... he is also under bondage to demonic powers who stalk the universe and who use the Law, not as a means of man's obedience to God, but as an instrument of their tyranny. This alienation of man from God is common to all mankind—it is neither purely Jewish nor purely Gentile. It is the state of man as child of Adam.[1]

Houlden goes on to explain that in Paul's worldview human beings need to be rescued from this bondage: "As far as the demonic powers are concerned, man's need is simply deliverance from their control." The key to this rescue is what Christ has done through his death and resurrection. This achieved a victory over sin, and the demonic powers of evil that bind humanity.

Although as Christians we still live in "this dark world" (Ephesians 6:12; compare with Philippians 2:15), does this mean we come under the power and control of Satan? No! For we have been transferred into Jesus' kingdom.

When Jesus reveals himself to Paul in a vision, and calls him to go to the Gentiles, the apostle is told that he will open people's eyes and "turn them from darkness to light, and from the power of Satan to

---

1. J. L. Houlden, *Paul's Letters from Prison*, p. 18.

God." (Acts 26:18) These words imply that people are under Satan's power before being saved by Christ, but through Christ they are redeemed from the power of evil and transferred out from the power of darkness into the Kingdom of God.

Paul explains in his letter to the Colossians how he prays for them:

> ... giving joyful thanks to the Father, who has qualified you to share in the inheritance of his holy people in the kingdom of light. For he has rescued us from the dominion of darkness and brought us into the kingdom of the Son he loves, in whom we have redemption, the forgiveness of sins. (Colossians 1:12-13)

When someone migrates to another country, they may apply for citizenship in their new country, but to do this they may have to renounce their former citizenship. Salvation in Christ is like this: when you enter the Kingdom of God you receive a new citizenship and you leave your old citizenship behind.

Your full transfer of allegiance to Jesus Christ needs to be intentional. This can include the following elements:

- Renounce Satan and all evil.
- Renounce all wrong ties to other people who have exercised ungodly authority over you.
- Renounce and break all ungodly covenants made by your ancestors on your behalf or which have impacted you in any way.
- Renounce all ungodly spiritual abilities which come through ungodly allegiances.
- Hand over the full rights of your life to Jesus Christ and invite him to rule in your heart as Lord from this day forward.

The battle

When a football player is transferred, he must play for his new team. He cannot play for his old team any more. It is like this when we are transferred into the Kingdom of God: we must play for Jesus' team and stop scoring goals for Satan's team.

According to the Bible a spiritual confrontation is going on between God and Satan. This is a cosmic civil rebellion against the Kingdom of God (Mark 1:15; Luke 10:18; Ephesians 6:12). It is a conflict between two kingdoms, in which there is no neutral ground for anyone to hide. Christians find themselves in an extended fight in which the decisive battle has already been won on the cross, and the final outcome is not in doubt: Christ has and will have the victory.

Followers of Christ are agents of Christ, so they now find themselves engaged in a daily battle with the powers of this dark age. Christ's death and resurrection provide our sole authority against this darkness and the basis of our power to stand against it. The contested territory of this warfare consists of people, communities, societies, and nations.

In this battle, even the church can be a battleground, and its resources can be exploited for evil purposes.

This is a serious and weighty matter. However, Paul describes the certainty of victory when he writes that the powers of this dark age have been disarmed, disgraced, and defeated through the cross and the forgiveness of sins that it won:

> When you were dead in your sins and in the uncircumcision of your sinful nature, God made you alive with Christ. He forgave us all our sins, having canceled the written code, with its regulations, that was against us and that stood opposed to us; he took it away, nailing it to the cross. And having disarmed the powers and authorities, he made a public spectacle of them, triumphing over them by the cross. (Colossians 2:13-15)

This passage uses an image from the Roman victory march called a 'triumph'. After defeating an enemy, a victorious general and his army would return to the city of Rome. To celebrate the victory, the general would lead a grand procession, in which the defeated enemies would be forced to march in chains through the streets of the city, their weapons and armor taken away from them. The people of Rome would look on, cheering the victors and jeering the defeated enemies.

Paul is using the Roman victory march image to explain the meaning of the cross. When Christ died for us, he canceled the power of sin. It is as if the accusations against us have been nailed to the cross: the cancellation of these accusations has been held up for all the powers of darkness to see. Because of this, Satan and his demonic powers, which seek to destroy us, have lost their power over us because they have no accusations to use against us. They have become like the enemies in the Roman victory march: defeated, disarmed, and publicly humiliated.

Through the cross, victory has been achieved over the powers and principalities of this dark age. This triumph plunders the evil powers and takes away their rights to rule, including those given to them through agreements into which people have entered, willingly or unwillingly, knowingly or unknowingly.

This is a powerful principle: for every tactic and accusation Satan uses against us, the cross provides the key to victory and freedom.

In the next two sections we consider Satan's role as the accuser, and the strategies he uses against people. After this we will examine six ways in which Satan tries to bind people, through sin, unforgiveness, words, wounds of the soul, lies (ungodly beliefs), and generational sin and resulting curses. For each strategy of Satan we will describe a remedy: a way for Christians to claim their freedom and break these influences off their lives. All of these issues will be important when we come to consider how to be set free from the bondages of Islam.

The accuser

Satan has strategies that he uses against us. It is good to know about and understand these strategies and be ready to stand against them. We need to apply and live out our freedom. For this we must pay attention: it is good for Christians to know and understand Satan's schemes, and be ready to resist them.

Paul writes in Ephesians 6:18 that Christians should "be alert." Likewise, Peter warns Christians to "Be alert and of sober mind. Your enemy the devil prowls around like a roaring lion looking for someone to devour." (1 Peter 5:8) What do we need to watch out for? We need to be alert to Satan's accusations.

The Bible calls Satan "the accuser" (Revelation 12:10) and in Hebrew the word 'satan' actually means 'accuser' or 'adversary'. This word was used for a legal opponent in a court of law. The word 'satan' is used this way in the Bible in Psalm 109: "let an accuser [a satan] stand on his right. When he is tried, let him be found guilty." (Psalm 109:6-7) In a similar scene Zechariah 3:1-3 refers to a figure called "the satan" who stands on the right hand of the high priest Joshua and accuses him before an angel of God. Another example is when Satan accuses Job before God (Job 1:9-11), asking permission to test him.

Whom does Satan accuse us *to*? We know that he accuses us before God. He also accuses us to others; and he accuses us to ourselves through the words of others and through our own thoughts. He wants us to be hurt by these accusations, to believe them, to be intimidated by them, and to be limited by them.

What does Satan accuse us of? He accuses us of our sins and he also accuses us for any parts of our lives that we have, in some way or other, surrendered to him.

We also need to understand that when Satan accuses us, his accusations are riddled with lies. Jesus said about Satan:

> He was a murderer from the beginning, not holding to the truth, for there is no truth in him. When he lies, he speaks his native language, for he is a liar and the father of lies. (John 8:44)

What are Satan's lying strategies, and how can we stand firm whenever he accuses us? It certainly helps if we know his strategies. For example, in 1 Corinthians, Paul urges Christians to practice forgiveness. Why is this important? Paul says that we forgive "in order that Satan might not outwit us. For we are not unaware of his schemes" (2 Corinthians 2:11). Paul is telling us that we can know what Satan is up to; and, because we know that one of Satan's strategies is to accuse us of unforgiveness, we will be quick to forgive others, so that we do not become vulnerable to his accusations.

Satan has other strategies as well. Here we will consider six of his main strategies to accuse believers, and consider how we can stand against them. These six strategies are:

- sin

- unforgiveness

- soul wounds

- words (and symbolic actions)

41

- ungodly beliefs (lies)
- generational sin and resulting curses.

As we shall see, a key step to finding spiritual freedom is to be able to name and reject all claims that Satan might make against us. This applies whether his accusations have some basis in truth or they are just complete lies.

Open doors and footholds

Before we consider each of these six areas, we need to introduce some useful names for the rights Satan claims against people, which he uses to oppress them. Two key names are 'open doors' and 'footholds.'

An open door is an entry point that someone may grant to Satan through ignorance, disobedience, or carelessness, and which Satan then exploits to attack and oppress the person. Let us recall Jesus' description of Satan as "the thief" who moves around looking for opportunities to steal, kill, and destroy (John 10:10). A safe home does not have doors left open: each door is securely locked.

A foothold is ground within the human soul that Satan claims a person has surrendered to him—a piece of us that Satan has marked as his own.

Paul refers to the possibility that a Christian could give opportunity to the devil by harboring anger: "In your anger do not sin: do not let the sun go down while you are still angry, and do not give the devil a foothold." (Ephesians 4:26-27) The Greek word translated "foothold" is *topos*, which means an 'inhabited place'. *Topos* has the core meaning of a place that is occupied, and the Greek expression "give a *topos* to" means to 'give opportunity to'. Paul is saying that if someone hangs on to anger, rather than confessing and renouncing it as a possible sin, they surrender spiritual ground to Satan. Satan can then occupy and use that ground for evil purposes. By holding on to anger, a person can give Satan a foothold.

In John 14, Jesus uses the language of legal rights when he states that Satan has no hold on him:

> I will not say much more to you, for the prince of this world is coming. He has no hold over me, but he comes so that the world

may learn that I love the Father and do exactly what my Father has commanded me. (John 14:30-31)

Archbishop J. H. Bernard writes in his commentary on this passage that Jesus is saying, "Satan … has no point in my personality on which he can fasten."[2] The idiom here is in fact a legal one, as is explained by D. A. Carson:

> He has no hold on me is an idiomatic rendering of "he has nothing in me," recalling a Hebrew idiom frequently used in legal contexts, meaning "he has no claim on me" or "he has nothing over me" … The devil could have a hold on Jesus only if there were a justifiable charge against Jesus.[3]

Why does Satan have no hold on Jesus? It is because Jesus is without sin. He says that he does "exactly what my Father has commanded me" (John 14:31; see also John 5:19). This is why there is nothing in Jesus that allows Satan to claim any legal rights over him. Jesus has no foothold that Satan can use.

Jesus was crucified as an innocent man. This is so important for the power of the cross. Because Jesus was innocent, Satan cannot claim that the crucifixion was a lawful penalty. The death of the Lord's Messiah was an innocent sacrifice on behalf of others, not a just penalty carried out against Jesus by Satan. If Christ had surrendered any ground to Satan, his death would have been a just punishment for sin. Instead, because Jesus was innocent, his death could be and is an effective offering for the sins of the whole world.

What can we do about open doors and footholds in our own lives? We can shut open doors, and remove footholds. To claim our spiritual freedom, these steps are essential. We need to do this systematically, closing all open doors and removing all footholds in our lives.

But how to do this? Let us consider each of six areas one by one. All will be important when we come to consider how Islam binds people.

---

2. J. H. Bernard, *A Critical and Exegetical Commentary on the Gospel According to John*, vol. 2, p. 556.
3. D. A. Carson, *The Gospel According to John*, pp. 508-9.

Sin

If the open door is sins we have committed, we can close this door by repenting of the sins by which we may have given permission for Satan to claim rights over our lives. The power of the cross is the key to this process. By appealing to Christ as Savior, we can receive God's forgiveness. As John writes, "the blood of Jesus ... purifies us from all sin" (1 John 1:7). If we are cleansed of sin, then sin has no power over us. As Paul writes, "we have been justified by his blood" (Romans 5:9). This means that God sees us as righteous. When we repent and turn to Christ, we are buried with him: we become identified with Jesus. Then we become someone against whom Satan can make no lawful charge. We become someone over whom Satan has no hold because our sin is "covered" (Romans 4:7). We are set free from his accusing claims against us.

How does this work in practice? If someone is struggling with a habit of persistent lying, then that person needs to be able to recognize that lying is wrong in God's sight, confess this, repent of lying, and be assured of forgiveness through the work of Christ. When this is done, lying itself can be rejected and renounced. If, on the other hand, the person likes lying, finds it useful, and has no intention of giving it up, any bid for freedom from lying is likely to be futile, and Satan will be able to use this foothold against the person.

We can close the door on sin by repenting, renouncing our sin, and trusting in the cross of Christ. In this way we deny Satan the right to use our sins against us.

Unforgiveness

Another strategy Satan likes to use against us is our unforgiveness. Forgiveness was something Jesus often taught about. He said that we will not be forgiven by God until we forgive others (Mark 11:25-26; Matthew 6:14-15).

Unforgiveness can tie us to someone's wrongdoing, or to a painful event. This can give Satan a foothold, a legal right against us. Paul writes about this in his second letter to the Corinthians:

Anyone you forgive, I also forgive. And what I have forgiven—if there was anything to forgive—I have forgiven in the sight of Christ for your sake, in order that Satan might not outwit us. For we are not unaware of his schemes. (2 Corinthians 2:10-11)

Why does our unforgiveness allow us to be outwitted by Satan? This is because he can use our unforgiveness as a foothold against us. But if we are "not unaware of his schemes," as Paul says, then we will know we need to remove his foothold through practicing forgiveness.

 There are three dimensions to forgiveness: forgiving others; receiving God's forgiveness; and sometimes also forgiving ourselves. This symbol of the Forgiveness Cross[4] helps us to remember these three aspects. The horizontal bar reminds us to forgive others. The vertical bar reminds us to receive God's forgiveness. The circle reminds us to forgive ourselves.

Forgiveness does not mean that we forget what the other person has done, or excuse it. It does not mean that we should just trust the person. Forgiving others means that we give up our right to accuse them before God. We release the person who has wronged us from any claim we might make against them. We hand them over to God to judge justly and we hand the issue over to God. Forgiveness is not a feeling: it is a decision.

It is important to receive forgiveness from God as well as give it, because forgiveness is all the more powerful when we know we have been forgiven (Ephesians 4:32).

There is a 'Forgiveness Prayer' in the Additional Resources section at the end of this training manual.

Soul wounds

A foothold can be caused by a wound in the soul. Wounds of the soul can actually hurt even more than wounds of the body, and when we are physically hurt, our soul can be wounded as well. Suppose

---

4. The Forgiveness Cross is from Chester and Betsy Kylstra, *Restoring the Foundations*, p. 98.

someone undergoes a traumatic and terrifying attack. After this they might suffer from fear for a long time. Satan can use that fear against the person to bind and enslave them to even more fear.

Once when I[5] was teaching on Islam, I was approached by a South African woman who had a traumatic experience involving people from a Muslim background a decade earlier. At the request of a local seminary, her family had offered hospitality to two men who had claimed to be converts from Islam. This was the start of an extremely difficult and hurtful time. Her house guests were aggressive and mocked her and her family continually. They would push her against the walls, call her a pig, curse he,r and even spit on her as they walked past. She even found small pieces of paper lodged in different places all around her home with curses written on them in Arabic. The family asked for help from their church, but no one would believe them. In the end they were only able to get rid of these 'guests' by renting alternative accommodation for them. The woman wrote, "At that time, we were financially, spiritually, emotionally and physically drained and rock bottom. I did not believe in myself any more, I felt I was good for nothing, because they treated me like dirt." After hearing me teach on Islamic bondages, she confronted the fears and self-doubt which had plagued her and rejected them. We prayed together for healing of the traumatic experiences, renouncing intimidation. She was wonderfully healed and said, "I praise the Lord for this heavenly appointment … I feel relieved and worthy to serve the Lord as a woman. Praise the Lord!" Later she wrote to me:

> We still serve the Lord, we love Him more than before, we learnt so much of the Muslim culture and beliefs and we became stronger through all of this and we can say that we love the Muslims with the love of the Lord and will never stop showing them through our lives, how much Jesus loves each one of them.

When people suffer soul wounds, Satan tries to feed lies to them. The lies are not true, but the person can believe them because the pain feels real. For this woman the lie was that she was worthless and "good for nothing."

To bring freedom from such lies, we can apply these five steps:

---

5. Mark Durie, the author of these lessons.

1. First invite the person to pour out their soul to the Lord, telling the Lord what they feel about their pain.

2. Then pray to Jesus to heal the trauma.

3. The person then forgives whoever had hurt them.

4. The person then renounces fear and other harmful effects of the trauma, declaring trust in God.

5. The person then confesses and rejects any lies they believed because of the hurt.

After this has been done, Satan's attacks can be much more successfully resisted as his foothold has been removed.

Words

Words can be very powerful. By using our words we can imprison others and ourselves. For this reason Satan tries to use our words against us. Jesus said:

> But I tell you that everyone will have to give account on the day of judgment for every empty word they have spoken. For by your words you will be acquitted, and by your words you will be condemned. (Matthew 12:36-37)

Jesus taught us to use our words for blessing, not cursing: "Love your enemies, do good to those who hate you, bless those who curse you, pray for those who mistreat you." (Luke 6:27-28)

The warning of Jesus not to speak careless words applies to all our speaking, including vows, promises, and spoken covenants we have entered into. Consider the reason Jesus gave to his disciples not to swear oaths:

> But I tell you, do not swear an oath at all… All you need to say is simply "Yes" or "No"; anything beyond this comes from the evil one. (Matthew 5:34, 37)

So why not swear oaths? Jesus explains that this comes from the "evil one," from Satan himself. Satan wants us to swear oaths because he plans to use our words against us, to harm us. It can give him a foothold in us, and a basis for him to accuse us. This can be true even if we have not understood the power of the words we have spoken.

What can we do, then, when we have sworn an oath or made a vow, promise, or covenant with words (and perhaps also ritual actions) which have bound us to a bad path, a path we should not have followed, and which is not God's way for us?

In Leviticus 5:4-10 there is an explanation of what the Israelites had to do when someone uttered a "careless oath" and they were bound because of their oath. A way was provided for being set free from this oath. The person had to bring a sacrifice to the priest, who would make atonement for this sin, and then the person would be released from their careless oath.

The good news is that because of the cross, we can be set free from ungodly promises, oaths, and vows we have made. It is wonderful that the Bible teaches us that the blood of Jesus "speaks a better word than the blood of Abel":

> But you have come to Mount Zion ... to Jesus the mediator of a new covenant, and to the sprinkled blood that speaks a better word than the blood of Abel. (Hebrews 12:22-24)

What this means is that the blood of Jesus has the power to cancel all curses against us due to words we have spoken. In particular, the covenant in Jesus' blood overrides and cancels all agreements we have made with fear or death.

Ritual acts: freedom from blood pacts

We have been discussing the power of words to bind us. In the Hebrew scriptures, a standard way of binding oneself in a covenant was by a blood pact. This involved words combined with a ritual action.

When God made his famous covenant with Abraham in Genesis 15, it was enacted through a sacrifice. Abraham provided the animal, slaughtered it, and laid the parts of the animal on the ground. Then a smoking flame—representing the presence and participation of God—passed along between the parts of the animal. This ritual invoked a curse to the effect of "may I become like this animal if I break this covenant"—that is, "may I be killed and cut into pieces."

This is reflected in the warning given by God through the prophet Jeremiah:

> Those who have violated my covenant and have not fulfilled the terms of the covenant they made before me, I will treat like the calf they cut in two and then walked between its pieces. The leaders of Judah and Jerusalem, the court officials, the priests and all the people of the land who walked between the pieces of the calf, I will deliver into the hands of their enemies who want to kill them. Their dead bodies will become food for the birds and the wild animals. (Jeremiah 34:18-20)

Initiation rituals, such as the rituals practiced in witchcraft, can involve binding a person in a pact through the use of blood sacrifice. In such rituals death may be invoked, not with actual blood, but symbolically: for example, by speaking curses of self-destruction; by wearing a symbol of death such as a noose around the neck; or by acting out death in a ritual, such as being placed in a coffin or undergoing a symbolic stabbing to the heart. (Later we will consider an example of this kind of ritual in connection with Islam.)

Blood pacts, including symbolic death rituals, invoke a curse of death upon the person and sometimes upon their descendants. This is spiritually dangerous because such rituals set up open doors for spiritual oppression. First they bind the person to the conditions of the pact, and then they establish spiritual permission for the person to be killed or to die, in fulfillment of the curses of the pact.

One Christian woman whose community has lived under Islamic rule for many generations was suffering from nightmares in which deceased relatives were beckoning to her to come to the land of the dead. She had also been plagued with completely illogical suicidal thoughts for which there was no apparent explanation. As I talked and prayed with her, it emerged that other members of her family, in previous generations, had also had inexplicable nightmares about death which troubled them greatly. I discerned that because her ancestors had lived under the Islamic rule, and were subject to the *dhimma* covenant of surrender, the fear of death was oppressing her. There was a specific ritual which her Christian male ancestors had to go through each year, when they paid the *jizya* tax to the Muslims in accordance with the conditions of the *dhimma*. As part of this ritual they were struck on the side of the neck to symbolize their decapitation if they broke the conditions of their pact of surrender to Islam. (We will discuss this ritual in Lesson 6.) I prayed with the woman against this, rebuking the power of death and canceling the specific curse of death tied to this decapitation ritual. After these prayers, which broke the power of this ritual, she experienced great relief from the nightmares and thoughts of death.

Ungodly beliefs (lies)

One of the main strategies that Satan uses against us is to feed us lies. When we accept and believe these lies, he can use them against us to accuse, confuse, and deceive us. Never forget that Satan is "a liar and the father of lies" (John 8:44). (In the story of the South African woman earlier in this lesson, the lie was that she was worthless.)

When we are becoming mature disciples of Jesus Christ, we learn how to identify and reject lies we had previously accepted as true. These lies or ungodly beliefs can show up in our lives in different ways: in what we say, in what we think and believe, and in our self-talk, which is what we think or say to ourselves when no one else is listening. Examples of ungodly beliefs are:

- "No one could ever love me."
- "People cannot change."
- "I will never be safe."
- "There is something fundamentally wrong with me."
- "If people find out what I am really like they will reject me."
- "God will never forgive me."

Some lies can be part of our community's culture; for example, "Women are weak," or "You cannot trust men." I am from an English (Anglo-Saxon) culture, and one of the lies in my culture is that it is wrong for men to show emotion. There is an English saying that "Real men don't cry." People call this "keeping a stiff upper lip." But this is not true: sometimes real men do cry!

As we grow into maturity as disciples, we learn to challenge the lies that are a part of our culture and replace them with the truth.

Remember: the most perfect lie is the one that *feels* true. Sometimes even if we know with our minds that an ungodly belief is not true, it can still feel true to our hearts.

Jesus has taught us, "If you hold to my teaching, you are really my disciples. Then you will know the truth, and the truth will set you free." (John 8:31-32)

The Holy Spirit helps us to identify and name the lies we have believed, and then to reject them (1 Corinthians 2:14-15). As we follow Jesus and learn to reject the world's lies, our thinking can be healed and transformed. Paul explains that in this way we can renew our minds:

> Do not conform to the pattern of this world, but be transformed by the renewing of your mind. Then you will be able to test and approve what God's will is—his good, pleasing and perfect will. (Romans 12:2)

The bad news is that lies can give Satan a foothold. The good news is that we can get rid of these footholds through a truth encounter. When we discern the truth we can confess, reject, and renounce any lies we had accepted.

There is a prayer to deal with lies in the Additional Resources section of this training manual.

Generational sins and resulting curses

Another strategy Satan can use against us is generational sin: the sins of our ancestors. These can come with curses which affect us badly.

We have all seen families where a particular sin or bad character is passed from one generation to another. There is an English proverb about this that says, "The apple does not fall far from the tree." Families can also pass on a spiritual inheritance which affects their descendants, by providing an open door for Satan. Spiritual oppression can affect multiple generations, as one generation binds the next by their sins and the resulting curses pass on evil from one generation to the next.

Some Christians find the concept of intergenerational spiritual bondage to be unacceptable or even irrational. They may point instead to the influence of parents' behaviors on children. For example, if a father is a liar, then his children could copy him, and learn to be liars too; or if a mother curses her child, the child could have a poor self-image as a result. This is learned behavior. But there is also a spiritual inheritance passed on by parents, which is distinct from this.

The whole worldview of the Bible in relation to covenants, curses, and blessings agrees with this view. The Bible describes how God made a covenant with the nation of Israel, dealing with them as an intergenerational community and binding them into a system of blessings and curses which applied to them and their descendants—the blessings to the thousandth generation, and the curses to the third or fourth generation (Exodus 20:5; 34:7).

Since God has dealt with people intergenerationally in this way, it is surely easy to understand that Satan claims intergenerational rights against humankind! Remember Satan is "the accuser" who "accuses them before our God day and night" (Revelation 12:10), throwing everything he can against us. He will and does accuse us because of our ancestors' sins. For example, Adam and Eve's sin unleashed intergenerational curses against their descendants, including pain in childbirth (Genesis 3:16); dominance of men over women (Genesis 3:16); hard labor to eke out a living (Genesis 3:17-18); and ultimately death and decay (Genesis 3:19). This is just how "this dark age" works. Satan knows it, and he uses it against us.

The Bible does prophesy a change in these affairs, when God will no longer hold people to account for their parents' sins, and each person will be responsible for their own sins:

> Yet you ask, "Why does the son not share the guilt of his father?" Since the son has done what is just and right and has been careful to keep all my decrees, he will surely live. The one who sins is the one who will die. The child will not share the guilt of the parent, nor will the parent share the guilt of the child. The righteousness of the righteous will be credited to them, and the wickedness of the wicked will be charged against them. (Ezekiel 18:19-20)

This passage is to be understood as a prophecy for the Messianic Age, the kingdom of Jesus Christ. This is not a fundamental change in the way "this dark world" works under Satan's rule, but a promise about a different world, a world transformed by the coming of the kingdom of the beloved Son of God. This is a promise, not only that under the new covenant God will deal with each person according to their own sins, but also that the power of Satan to bind people through their parents' and ancestors' sins will be broken by the power of the death and resurrection of Jesus Christ.

So although it is true that the covenant of the old law, the "law of sin and death," did speak of sins being passed on from one generation to another, Christ has set aside this old law, by which Satan claimed rights to bind people to their parents' sins, making it null and void through the cross. This is a freedom that Christians have every right to claim for themselves.

How then can we claim our freedom from generational curses? The answer is found in the Bible. The Torah explains that for succeeding generations to be free of the effects of their ancestors' sins, they need to "confess their sins and the sins of their ancestors" (Leviticus 26:40). Then, God says, he will "remember the covenant with their ancestors" and heal them and their land (Leviticus 26:45).

We can use the same strategy. We can:

- confess our ancestor's sins and our own sins,
- reject and renounce these sins, and then
- break all curses caused by these sins.

We have authority to do this because of the cross of Christ. The cross has the power to set us free from every curse: "Christ redeemed us from the curse of the law by becoming a curse for us ..." (Galatians 3:13)

There is a 'Prayer for Generational Sin' in the Additional Resources section of this training manual.

In the following sections we will consider the authority we have in Christ and how to apply it to our specific situation. We will also describe five steps to defeat Satan's strategies.

Our kingdom authority

Jesus himself instructed the disciples that they had power to "bind" and "loose" affairs in the heavens and upon the earth, which is to say, in both the spiritual realm and the physical domain:

> I tell you the truth, whatever you bind on earth will be [or has been] bound in heaven, and whatever you loose on earth will be [or has been] loosed in heaven. (Matthew 18:18; see also 16:19)

The promise of our authority over Satan is actually announced at the beginning of the Bible in Genesis 3:15 where God tells the serpent that the offspring of the woman will "crush your head." Paul speaks of this too: "The God of peace will soon crush Satan under your feet." (Romans 16:20)

When Jesus sent out his disciples, first twelve and then seventy-two, he gave them authority to drive out demons while proclaiming the Kingdom of God (Luke 9:1). Later, when the disciples returned, they expressed their amazement at this authority, saying, "Lord, even the demons submit to us in your name." Jesus replied, "I saw Satan fall like lightning from heaven." (Luke 10:17-18)

It is a wonderful comfort that Christians do have the authority to defeat and destroy Satan's strategies. This means that believers have authority to break and cancel ungodly pacts and vows because the covenant in the blood of Christ cancels the power of every pact made for evil purposes. This is a promise reflected in prophecies about the Messiah in Zechariah:

> As for you, because of the blood of my covenant with you, I will free your prisoners from the waterless pit. (Zechariah 9:11)

The principle of specificity

When pursuing freedom, it is necessary to take specific actions that counteract and deal with ungodly open doors and footholds. The Old Testament commands that idols and their places of worship must be completely destroyed. A model of how to ransack the idols' spiritual territory is provided in Deuteronomy 12:1-3, in which God commanded his people to completely and thoroughly destroy the high places (worship places), ritual sites, ritual objects, and altars, together with the idols themselves.

It is good and helpful to name one's sins specifically in confession. In the same way, when we claim our spiritual freedom we should also be specific. This shines the light of God's truth into each and every area that needs forgiveness. Where ungodly pacts have been entered into, they need to be revoked one by one, together with each of their conditions and consequences. This needs to be specific. In general, the more powerful the strategy Satan uses, the more specific we need to be when breaking its power.

This *principle of specificity* applies when we choose to free ourselves from ungodly commitments we have made by our words and actions. For example, a person who has bound themselves to a vow of silence through a blood sacrifice needs to repent of and renounce participation in this ritual and specifically annul their vow made through it. Likewise, someone struggling from unforgiveness who has uttered such words as "I will never forgive so-and-so as long as I live" must repent of this vow, renounce this commitment, and ask for God's forgiveness for uttering it. A victim of sexual abuse who has agreed to remain silent on threat of harm or death needs to renounce their vow of silence in order to claim their freedom: for example, "I renounce my silence about what has been done to me, and claim the right to speak out."

A woman called Susan had lost a number of people she loved: her father, her mother, and her husband. She was afraid that if she loved someone she would lose them as well, so she vowed to herself, "I will never love anyone else again." After this she became very bitter and hostile to others. She would swear and curse anyone who came near her. But when she was in her eighties she found Jesus and joined a church. This gave her hope and she renounced her 50-year-old vow never to love again. Set free from fear, she made deep and beautiful friendships with other women in the church. Her life was completely changed as Satan's grip on her life was broken.

Five steps to freedom

Here is a simple ministry model involving five steps which can be used to oppose and destroy Satan's strategies against us.

55

1. Confess and repent

A first step is to confess any sin, and also to declare the truth of God that applies to this issue. For example, if you have held an ungodly belief, you can confess this specifically as a sin, ask God's forgiveness for this, and repent of the sin. You can also declare God's truth that applies in this situation.

2. Renounce

The next step is to renounce. This means to publicly declare that you no longer support, believe in, agree with, or have any connection with something. For example, if you have participated in an ungodly ritual, when you renounce that ritual, you withdraw or revoke your previous commitment to it. As explained previously it is important to do this specifically.

3. Break

This step involves taking authority in the spiritual realm to break the power of something. For example, if there has been a curse involved, you can declare, "I break this curse." Jesus' disciples have been given "authority over all the power of the enemy" in Jesus' name (Luke 10:19). Breaking also should be done specifically.

4. Cast out

When demons have taken advantage of a foothold or an open door to afflict a person, once you have dealt with any open doors or footholds, removing them by confessing, renouncing, and breaking, you should command the demons to leave.

5. Bless and fill

The final step is to bless the person and pray that God will fill them with every good thing, including the opposite to what has afflicted them. For example, if they were struggling with fear of death, bless them with life and courage.

These five steps can be used for all kinds of bondages, but our focus here is freedom from Islam, so in later lessons we will learn how to use these steps to set people free from the bondages of Islam.

Study Guide

Lesson 2

Vocabulary

renounce	open doors	self-talk
freedom	footholds	truth encounter
Messiah	*topos*	soul wounds
Satan	legal rights	generational sin
Kingdom of God	Forgiveness Cross	spiritual inheritance
this dark age	oath	intergenerational
Roman triumph	blood pact	principle of
footholds	*jizya*	specificity

New names

- The Reverend J. L. Houlden: Fellow of Trinity College Oxford (born 1929)

- The Reverend J. H. Bernard: Irish Anglican Bishop (1860-1927)

- D. A. Carson: Professor of New Testament (born 1946)

Bible in this lesson

Romans 8:21

Isaiah 61:1-2

Luke 4:18-21

John 10:10; 8:44

Colossians 1:13

John 12:31

2 Corinthians 4:4

Ephesians 2:2

1 John 5:19

Ephesians 6:12

Philippians 2:15

Acts 26:18

Colossians 1:12-13

Mark 1:15

Luke 10:18

Colossians 2:13-15

Ephesians 6:18

1 Peter 5:8

Revelation 12:10

Psalm 109:6-7

Zechariah 3:1-3

Job 1:9-11

2 Corinthians 2:11

Ephesians 4:26-27

John 14:30-31; 5:19

Mark 11:25-26

Matthew 6:14-15

2 Corinthians 2:10-11

Ephesians 4:32

Matthew 12:36-37

Luke 6:27-28

Matthew 5:34, 37

Leviticus 5:4-10

Hebrews 12:22-24

Genesis 15

Jeremiah 34:18-20

John 8:31-32

1 Corinthians 2:14-15

Romans 12:2

Exodus 20:5; 34:7

Revelation 12:10

Genesis 3:16-19

Ezekiel 18:19-20

Leviticus 26:40, 45

Galatians 3:13

Matthew 18:18

Matthew 16:19

Genesis 3:15

Romans 16:20

Luke 10:17-18

1 John 1:7   Zechariah 9:11

Romans 5:9; 4:7   Deuteronomy 12:1-3

Questions Lesson 2

- Discuss the case study.

1. What surprised Reza when he tried to pray a prayer **renouncing** Islam?

2. After he managed to pray the prayer, what changed in Reza's life?

Jesus starts to teach

3. What is the birthright of every Christian?

4. Where did Jesus start to teach publicly?

5. What promise did he say he came to fulfill?

6. What things did Jesus set people free from?

A time to choose

7. A prisoner's prison door is left unlocked. What does the prisoner have to do if he wants to enjoy his **freedom**? What does this tell us about spiritual **freedom**?

Satan and his kingdom

8. What are some of the titles of **Satan** and what do they teach us?

9. Based on John 12:31 and other verses listed with it, what does Durie concede Satan has but in limited form?

10. What does Durie instruct us to assess in Islam?

The great transfer

11. According to Colossians 1:12-13 and **J. L. Houlden**, human nature is in bondage to which power?

12. According to Acts 26:18, from which powers are people saved, redeemed, and transferred?

13. According to Paul, when God rescues us, what happens to us?

14. What does Paul want the Colossians to be grateful for?

15. What are five aspects of transferring our full allegiance to Jesus Christ?

The battle

16. Based on Mark 1:15 and other verses listed with it, in what confrontation do Christians find themselves?

17. What cautious word does Durie speak over the church in the daily engagement with evil powers?

18. In this battle, what can Christians be certain of, according to Paul?

19. How does Paul use the idea of the **Roman triumph** to explain the victory of the cross?

The accuser

20. What does the Hebrew word *satan* mean?

21. In the light of **Satan**'s activities what do both Peter and Paul warn Christians to do?

22. What does **Satan** accuse us of?

23. What are the six strategies Durie lists that **Satan** uses to accuse us?

24. What is a key step in finding spiritual **freedom**?

Open doors and footholds

25. How does Durie define:

   ▪ an open door and
   ▪ a foothold?

26. If we refuse to confess and renounce sin, what might we be surrendering to **Satan**?

27. What do Christ's words "he has no hold on me" mean?

28. What could **Satan** not find in Jesus to claim?

29. Why is it important that Jesus was crucified as an innocent man?

Sin

30. What do we need to do with **open doors** and **footholds**?

31. How do we close the **open door** of sin in our life?

Unforgiveness

32. According to Jesus, what is the condition for being forgiven?

33. Why does our unforgiveness allow **Satan** to outwit us?

34. What are the three dimensions of forgiveness?

35. If we forgive does this mean we must also forget?

Soul wounds

36. How does **Satan** use **soul wounds** against us?

37. From what did a South African woman find healing, and what did she need to **renounce**?

38. What five steps are needed if a **foothold** is a wound in the soul?

Words

39. According to Matthew 12, what will we have to give account for on Judgment Day?

40. Why does **Satan** want us to swear **oaths**?

41. What has the power to cancel the destructive power of our spoken words?

Ritual acts: freedom from blood pacts

42. What does the **blood pact** that Abraham made with God in Genesis 15 imply? (Also consider Jeremiah 34:18-20.)

43. Why are **blood pacts** dangerous?

44. What was symbolized by the blow on the neck of Christians living under Islam, when they paid the annual *jizya* tax to Muslims?

Ungodly beliefs (lies)

45. What is one of Satan's main strategies to damage us?

46. What does Durie say we need to do in order to become mature disciples of Christ?

47. What does Durie say is a lie that is part of English culture?

48. According to Durie, what is the "most perfect lie"?

49. What actions and what kind of "encounter" enable us to close the door on **Satan**'s lies?

Generational sin and resulting curses

50. What does Durie believe can be passed on from one generation to another in a family, just as genetics are passed on to children?

51. What does Durie argue cannot fully explain the range of spiritual oppression that certain people experience?

52. Into which system did God bind the Israelite people as a whole in his covenant with them? (See Exodus 20:5; 34:7.)

53. As an example of an **intergenerational** legacy, what did Adam and Eve's sin unleash? (See Revelation 12:10, Genesis 3:16-19.)

54. How does Durie reply to the declaration in Ezekiel 18 that sons do not carry the sins of their fathers?

55. What three steps can be used to deal with the effects of **generational sin?**

Our kingdom authority

56. What authority is promised to humankind in Genesis 3:15 and then delivered to the disciples by Jesus, according to Matthew 16:19 and 18:18, in fulfillment of Zechariah 9:11?

The principle of specificity

57. Why is the instruction concerning idols in the Old Testament a model for how spiritual territories must be addressed? (See Deuteronomy 12:1-3.)

58. What has the power to break and cancel the power of evil pacts we might have entered into?

59. What kinds of actions does Durie say we need to take when dealing with open doors and footholds?

60. What was the inner vow made by Susan? What consequences did it bring in her life? How was she set free from that vow?

Five steps to freedom

61. What are the five steps to freedom? Can you commit them to memory?

62. What is the confession and what is the declaration needed to claim one's freedom?

63. According to Durie, what should you bless a person with once they have been set free?

3

Understanding Islam

"Then you will know the truth and the truth will set you free."
John 8:32

Lesson objectives

a. Understand the role of submission in becoming a Muslim.

b. Appreciate the governing role of Muhammad's personality in a Muslim's submission to Allah.

c. Understand why it is essential to have *sharia* laws to guide Muslims.

d. See how 'success' and 'losing' shape Muslim convictions.

e. Describe the four types of people as seen from the Quran.

f. Understand Muhammad's and Islam's teachings on Christians and Jews.

g. Recognize the implications that the most repeated Muslim prayer has for Christians and Jews.

h. Consider the damage caused by *sharia* laws.

i. Clarify why deception is permitted in Islam.

j. Encourage Christians to inform themselves about a faith that is guarded by experts.

k. Distinguish between Isa, the Islamic Jesus, and the real Jesus of history.

Case study: What would you do?

After much prayer, you and your church team feel led by the Spirit to start a house church in a new subdivision where many Muslims live. After several months of discreetly meeting with family and neighbors in the home of a man called "a man of peace" (Luke 10:6), the host informs you after a meeting that he and you are both summoned to meet the local community mayor. When you arrive there, you find that an imam and several mosque elders are present. You shake hands. You find out quickly that they accuse you of disturbing the peace by holding clandestine meetings in which you insult their prophet Muhammad. Both you and your host deny this strongly. The imam then says, "You Christians do not believe in Allah and you reject his final prophet Muhammad. You will go to hell. Allah considers Muslims superior and we must rule over you. If you do not submit to Islam, we are mandated to resist you, and even Isa will fight against you when he returns to earth. You must cease and desist from forcing vulnerable people in our community into your corrupted religion." You do not know the religion of the mayor, but he looks at you as if to say that you are permitted to reply to this accusation.

What will you say?

––––––––

In these sections we introduce the *shahada* and explain how it ties Muslims to follow the example of Muhammad.

How to become a Muslim

The word *Islam* is Arabic, meaning 'surrender' or 'submission'. The word *Muslim* means a 'submitter', someone who has surrendered to Allah.

What does this surrender and submission mean? The dominant picture of Allah in the Quran is the sovereign master who has absolute authority over all things. The expected attitude to take toward this master is to submit to his authority.

71

Someone who enters Islam agrees to submit to Allah and to the ways of his messenger. This agreement is done by confessing the *shahada*, the Islamic creed:

Ashhadu an la ilaha illa Allah,
wa ashhadu anna Muhammadun Rasulu Allah

I confess that there is no god but Allah,
and I confess that Muhammad is Allah's messenger.

If you accept the *shahada* and recite it for yourself, you have become a Muslim.

Although these are just a few words, their implications are vast. Reciting the *shahada* is a covenant declaration that Muhammad will be your guide for life. Being a Muslim—a 'submitter'—means following Muhammad as the unique, final messenger of Allah, who provides guidance for every detail of life.

The guidance of Muhammad is found in two sources, which together comprise the Islamic canon:

- The *Quran* is a book of revelations given to Muhammad from Allah.

- The *Sunna* is the example of Muhammad, which includes:

   - teachings: the things Muhammad taught people to do

   - actions: the things Muhammad did.

The example of Muhammad (the *Sunna*) is reported for Muslims in two main forms. One is in collections of *hadiths*, which are traditional sayings believed to report what Muhammad did and said. The other is in the *siras*, which are biographies of Muhammad which claim to tell the story of his life from start to finish.

Muhammad's personality

Anyone who is bound by the *shahada* is obligated to follow Muhammad's example and emulate his character. All this follows from the *shahada*'s confession that Muhammad is Allah's messenger. Reciting these words in the *shahada* means you have accepted Muhammad's guidance for your life and you are bound to follow him.

In the Quran, Muhammad is called the best example, obligatory for all to follow:

> Surely Allah's messenger has been a good example for you, for one who hopes in Allah and the Last Day and remembers Allah often. (Q33:21)

> Whoever obeys the messenger has obeyed Allah ... (Q4:80)

> It is not for a believing man or woman, when Allah and his messenger have decided a matter, to have the choice in their affair. Whoever disobeys Allah and his messenger has very clearly gone astray. (Q33:36)

The Quran states that those who follow Muhammad will be successful and blessed:

> Whoever obeys Allah and his messenger, and fears Allah and guards [themselves] from him, they are the triumphant. (Q24:52)

> Whoever obeys Allah and the messenger are with those whom Allah has blessed ... (Q4:69)

Opposing Muhammad's instruction and example is said to be disbelief which leads to failure in this life and the fire in the next. These curses are laid upon Muslims in the Quran:

> But whoever breaks with the messenger after the guidance has become clear to him, and follows a way other than the believers' way, we [Allah] will turn over to what he has turned to and will burn him in hell, an evil destination! (Q4:115)

> Whatever the messenger gives you, receive it and whatever he forbids you, refrain from it. Protect yourselves from Allah. Surely Allah is harsh in retribution. (Q59:7)

The Quran even commands fighting against anyone who rejects Muhammad:

> Fight those who do not believe in Allah and the Last Day and do not forbid what Allah and his messenger have forbidden—who do not practice the religion of truth among those who have been given the Book—until they pay the tribute out of hand and are disgraced. (Q9:29)

... so make the believers firm. I shall cast terror into the unbelievers' hearts; so strike them over the neck and strike every one of their fingers! Because they broke with Allah and with his messenger, and whoever breaks with Allah and with his messenger, surely Allah is harsh in retribution. (Q8:12-13)

But is Muhammad's example worth following? While some aspects of Muhammad's life are positive, others are admirable, and many are fascinating, there are things Muhammad did that are wrong by almost any ethical standard. Numerous actions of Muhammad in the *siras* and the *hadiths* are shocking, including acts of murder, torture, rape and other abuses of women, enslavement, theft, deception, and incitement against non-Muslims.

Such material is not only disturbing as evidence of who Muhammad the individual was: through the *sharia* it also has implications for all Muslims. Muhammad's example was legislated by Allah in the Quran as the best model to follow, so all incidents in Muhammad's life, even the bad ones, become standards for Muslims to follow.

The Quran—Muhammad's personal document

Observant Muslims believe the Quran to be the letter-perfect revelation of Allah's guidance to humanity, delivered through his messenger Muhammad. If you accept the messenger, you must accept his message. The *shahada* therefore obligates a Muslim to believe in and obey the Quran.

A key thing to grasp about the way the Quran was produced is that Muhammad and the Quran are as intimately interconnected as a body is to its backbone. The *Sunna*—Muhammad's teaching and example—is like the body and the Quran the backbone. Neither can stand without the other, and you cannot comprehend one without the other.

The Islamic *sharia*—the 'way' to be a Muslim

To follow the teaching and example of Muhammad, a Muslim must look to the Quran and the *Sunna*. However, this raw material is too complex and difficult for most Muslims to access, understand, and use for themselves. It became obvious to religious leaders in the early Islamic centuries that the majority of Muslims must rely on a small number of experts who could classify and organize the raw materials of Muhammad's *Sunna* and the Quran into a systematic and consistent set of rules for living. So, based on the Quran and the *Sunna* of Muhammad, Muslim jurists put together what came to be known as the *sharia*, the 'path' or 'way' to live as a Muslim.

The Islamic *sharia* can also be referred to as the *sharia* of Muhammad, because it is based upon Muhammad's example and teaching. The *sharia* system of rules defines a total way of life, for both the individual and the community. There can be no Islam without *sharia*.

Because Muhammad's *Sunna* is a foundation of *sharia* law, it is important to understand and pay attention to the recorded details of what Muhammad did and said as recorded in the *hadiths* and the *sira*. Ignorance about Muhammad is ignorance about the *sharia*, and that is ignorance about the human rights of people who live under Islamic conditions or whose lives are influenced by Islam. What Muhammad did, *sharia* law commends to Muslims to emulate, and the lives of all are affected, both Muslims and non-Muslims. The relationship between Muhammad's life and the lives of Muslim people today may not always be a direct one, but it remains extremely powerful and significant.

Another thing to note about the *sharia* is that, in contrast to the laws made by parliaments, which are devised by people and can be changed, the *sharia* is thought to be divinely mandated. It is therefore claimed that the *sharia* is perfect and unchangeable. Nevertheless, there are some areas of flexibility. New circumstances keep arising for which Muslim jurists must work out how the *sharia* is to be applied, but these are adjustments around the edges of what is regarded as a pre-ordained, perfect, and timeless system.

In these next sections we examine Islam's teaching that Muslims are the successful ones, who are superior to other people.

"Come to success"

According to the Quran, what is the result of right guidance? For those who submit to Allah and accept his guidance, the intended result is *success* in this life and the next. The call of Islam is a call to success.

This call to success is proclaimed in the *adhan*, or call to worship, which sounds forth to Muslims five times a day:

> Allah is Greater! Allah is Greater!
> Allah is Greater! Allah is Greater!
> I witness that there is no god but Allah.
> I witness that there is no god but Allah.
> I witness that Muhammad is the messenger of Allah.
> I witness that Muhammad is the messenger of Allah.
> Come to worship. Come to worship.
> **Come to success. Come to success.**
> Allah is Greater! Allah is Greater!
> Allah is Greater! Allah is Greater!
> There is no god but Allah.

The Quran emphasizes the importance of success a great deal. It divides humanity into winners and the rest. Those who do not accept Allah's guidance are repeatedly called 'losers':

> Whoever desires any religion other than Islam, it shall not be accepted from him and in the next world he shall be one of the **losers**. (Q3:85)

> If you associate [say that Allah shares his power or rule with another], your works shall amount to nothing, and you will be one of the **losers**. (Q39:65)

Islam's emphasis on success and failure means that many Muslims have been taught by their religion to regard themselves as superior to non-Muslims, and more pious Muslims are told they are superior to less pious Muslims, so discrimination is a way of life in Islam.

A divided world

Throughout its chapters, the Quran has much to say, not only about Muslims, but about people of other faiths as well, including a lot about Christians and Jews. The Quran and Islamic legal terminology make reference to four different categories of people:

1. First and foremost there are the *genuine Muslims*.

2. Then there is another category called *hypocrites*, who are rebellious Muslims.

3. *Idolaters* were the dominant category among the Arabs before Muhammad appeared. The Arabic word for idolater is *mushrik*, which literally means 'associator'. These are people who are thought to have committed *shirk* 'association', which means saying that anyone or anything is like Allah, or that Allah has partners who share in his power and reign.

4. The *People of the Book* are a subcategory of *mushrik*. This category includes Christians and Jews. They must be considered *mushrik*, because the Quran names both Christians and Jews as being guilty of *shirk* (Q9:30-31; Q3:64).

The concept of the People of the Book signifies that Christianity and Judaism are believed to be related to and derived from Islam. Islam is regarded as the mother religion from which Christians and Jews diverged over the centuries. According to the Quran, Christians and Jews follow a faith that was originally pure monotheism—in other words, Islam—but their scriptures have been corrupted and are no longer authentic. In this sense, Christianity and Judaism are regarded as distorted derivatives of Islam whose followers have gone astray from the rightly guided path.

The Quran includes both positive and negative comments about Christians and Jews. On the positive side it reports that some Christians and Jews are faithful and believe truly (Q3:113-14). However, the same chapter says the test of their sincerity is that the genuine ones will become Muslims (Q3:199).

According to Islam, Christians and Jews could not be freed from their ignorance until Muhammad came bringing the Quran (Q98:1). Islam teaches that Muhammad was Allah's gift to Christians and Jews to correct misunderstandings. This means Christians and Jews should accept Muhammad as Allah's messenger, and the Quran as his final revelation (Q4:47; Q5:15; Q57:28-29).

Here are four claims that the Quran and the *Sunna* make about non-Muslims, and about Christians and Jews in particular:

1. Muslims are "the best people" and superior to other peoples. Their role is to instruct them concerning what is right and wrong, commanding what is right and forbidding what is wrong (Q3:110).

2. Islam's destiny is to rule over all other religions (Q48:28).

3. To achieve this ascendancy, Muslims are to fight against Jews and Christians (the People of the Book) until they are defeated and humbled, and forced to pay tribute to the Muslim community (Q9:29).

4. Christians and Jews who cling to their *shirk* and continue to disbelieve in Muhammad and his monotheism—that is, those who do not convert to Islam—will go to hell (Q5:72; Q4:47-56).

Although Jews and Christians are considered together to form the one category known as the People of the Book, the Jews are criticized more. In the Quran and the *Sunna*, numerous specific theological claims are made against them. For example, Muhammad taught that at the end, the very stones will lend their voices to help Muslims kill the Jews, and the Quran says that it is Christians who are "nearest in love" to Muslims, but Jews (and idolaters) have the greatest enmity against Muslims (Q5:82).

In the end, however, the Quran's final verdict is negative on both Jews and Christians alike. This condemnation is even incorporated into the daily prayers of every observant Muslim.

Jews and Christians in Muslims' daily prayers

The best-known chapter (*sura*) of the Quran is *al-Fatihah* 'the Opening'. This *sura* is recited as part of all the mandatory daily prayers—the *salat*—and repeated within each prayer. Faithful Muslims who say all their prayers recite this *sura* at least 17 times a day, and over 5,000 times a year.

Al-Fatihah is a prayer for guidance:

In the name of Allah,
the merciful, the compassionate.
Praise be to Allah, the Lord of the worlds,

the merciful, the compassionate,
the master of the day of judgment.
It is you whom we worship
and it is you whom we ask for help.
Guide us to the straight path,
the path of those whom you have blessed,
not of **those on whom your anger falls**,
nor of **those who go astray.** (Q1:1-7)

This is a prayer asking Allah's help to lead the believer along the "straight path." As such it is true to the heart of Islam's message of guidance.

But who are those who are said to have fallen under the anger of Allah, or gone astray from the straight path? Who are these people who deserve to be spoken about so badly in every Muslim's prayers, each day, hundreds of thousands of times in many Muslims' lifetimes? Muhammad clarified the meaning of this *sura*, saying, "Those who have earned the anger are the Jews and those who are led astray are the Christians."

It is remarkable that the daily prayers of every Muslim, at the very core of Islam, include a rejection of Christians and Jews as misguided and objects of Allah's wrath.

In these next sections we consider the damage caused by the Islamic *sharia*. This is ultimately due to Muhammad's example and teaching.

Problems of the *sharia*

When Islam becomes established in a country, over a long time the culture of the community can be reshaped by the *sharia*. This process is called 'Islamization'. Because there were so many things that were not good in the life and teaching of Muhammad, many injustices and social problems are brought by the *sharia*. This means that although Islam promises success, *sharia* societies often cause a lot of harm to people. If we look around the world today, we can see that many Islamic countries are poorly developed and have many human rights issues due to the influence of Islam.

Some of the injustices and problems caused by the *sharia* are:

- Women have inferior status in Muslim societies and suffer many abuses due to Islamic law. We will consider an example: the case of Amina Lawal below.

- Islam's teaching of *jihad* has been causing conflict and harm to millions of men, women, and children all over the world.

- The *sharia*'s punishments for certain crimes are cruel and excessive: for example, cutting off the hand of thieves and killing apostates for rejecting Islam.

- The *sharia* is not able to change people to make them good. When Islamic revolutions have happened in countries, and radical Muslims have taken over the government, the result has been more corruption, not less. The recent history of Iran is an example: after the Iranian Islamic Revolution in 1978, when the Shah was overthrown, Muslim scholars took over the government but, despite their promises, corruption only increased.

- Muhammad allowed and even encouraged Muslims to lie in certain circumstances. We will discuss the consequences of this later.

- Because of Islamic teachings, non-Muslims are often discriminated against in Muslim societies. Most persecution of Christians in the world today is done by Muslims.

The case of Amina Lawal

Now we will consider an example of a Muslim woman whose life was threatened by the *sharia*. In 1999 Nigeria introduced *sharia* courts for Muslim majority states in the north of the country. Three years later, in 2002, Amina Lawal was sentenced to death by stoning by a *sharia* judge because she had given birth to a child conceived after her divorce. She gave the name of the father of the child, but without a DNA test the court could not prove that he was the father, so the man was found not guilty. Only the woman was convicted of adultery and sentenced to be stoned.

The judge who convicted Amina also ruled that her stoning should not happen until after she had weaned her child. This sentence, and applying it after the child was weaned, closely followed the example of Muhammad, who had a Muslim woman stoned to death after she confessed to adultery, but only after the child was weaned and eating solid food.

The *sharia* stoning law is bad for several reasons:

- It is excessive.
- It is cruel: death by stoning is a horrible way to die.
- It also damages the men who do the stoning.
- It is discriminatory, targeting a woman who becomes pregnant but not the man who causes her to become pregnant.
- It deprives a young infant of its mother, making it an orphan.
- It ignores the possibility that a woman could have been raped.

Amina's case attracted international outrage. More than a million letters of protest were sent to Nigerian embassies around the world. Fortunately for Amina, her sentence was overturned by a court of appeal. In overturning Amina's sentence the *sharia* appeal court did not actually reject the principle that the Islamic penalty for adultery is stoning to death. Other reasons were given instead; for example, the court of appeal stated that there should have been three judges passing Amina's sentence, not just one.

Lawful deception

One of the problematic aspects of the Islamic *sharia* is its teachings on lying and deception. While it must be acknowledged that lying is considered a very serious sin in Islam, there are situations where lying is permissible or even compulsory, according to Islamic authorities, based upon Muhammad's example.

There are several distinct circumstances in which Muslims are permitted or required to lie. For example, there is a chapter in the collection of *hadiths* called *Sahih al-Bukhari* which has the heading "He who makes peace between people is not a liar." According to this aspect of Muhammad's example, one of the circumstances in which Muslims are permitted to say untrue things is when lying to help reconcile people will have a positive effect.

Another context for lawful lying is when Muslims are in danger from non-Muslims (Q3:28). From this verse is derived the concept of *taqiyya,* which refers to the practice of deception in order to keep Muslims safe. The consensus of Muslim scholars has been that Muslims, when living under the political dominance of non-Muslims, are allowed to show friendliness and kindness to non-Muslims as a protective measure, so long as they hold fast to their faith (and enmity) in their hearts. One implication of this doctrine is that observant Muslims' behavior toward non-Muslims might be expected to become less friendly, and their beliefs less veiled, as their political power increases.

Other circumstances where *sharia* law encourages Muslims to lie include: between husbands and wives to maintain marital harmony; when resolving disputes; when telling the truth might cause you to incriminate yourself—Muhammad sometimes would rebuke people who confessed to a crime; when someone has entrusted you with their secret; and in warfare. More generally, Islam advocates an ethic for lying in which the end justifies the means.

Some Muslim scholars have made fine distinctions between different kinds of lies; for example, giving a misleading impression is preferred to telling a plain lie. Utilitarian—'the end justifies the means'—ethics for lying and truth-telling can cause a lot of harm to a society. This destroys trust and creates confusion, damaging domestic and political cultures. The Muslim *Umma*—the whole community of Muslims—is an ethically damaged community because of this. For example, if husbands habitually lie to their wives to smooth over differences, as Muhammad taught, this will erode trust within marriage. If children observe their fathers lying to their mothers this will give them permission to lie to others, and make it harder for them to trust other people. A culture of lawful deception causes a breakdown of trust across the whole society. This means, for example, that conducting business is more expensive, conflicts are prolonged, and reconciliation is much harder to achieve.

When someone leaves Islam, it is important that they specifically renounce this aspect of Muhammad's example. We will come back to this in Lesson 7.

Think for yourself

Because of the way knowledge is organized and even guarded in Islam, it can be difficult to know what Islam really teaches on certain subjects. A culture of lying can make this problem worse.

The primary sources of Islam are large and complex, and the process of deriving *sharia* rulings from the source materials of the Quran and the *Sunna* is considered to be a highly skilled one, requiring long years of training, which the vast majority of Muslims are not able to undertake. This means that Muslims must rely on their scholars for guidance in matters of faith. Indeed, Islamic law instructs Muslims to seek out someone who is more knowledgeable about matters of faith than themselves, and to follow that person. If Muslims have questions about *sharia* law, they are supposed to ask someone who has the required expertise.

Islamic religious knowledge is not democratized in the way biblical knowledge has been in recent centuries. It is made available on a need-to-know basis. In Islam certain things are just not discussed if there is no need to mention them and if it might put Islam in a bad light to do so. Many Muslims have had the experience of being rebuked when they ask their Islamic teacher the 'wrong question'.

No one should let themselves be intimidated by claims that they have no right to express opinions about Islam, the Quran, or the *Sunna* of Muhammad. In this age, when primary source material is easily available on these subjects, everyone—Christians, Jews, atheists, or Muslims—should take every opportunity to inform themselves, and speak out their views on these matters. Anyone and everyone who is affected by Islam has the right to inform themselves and form their own opinions about it.

In these next sections we discuss Islam's understanding of Jesus, and explain why the Islamic Jesus cannot provide human beings with freedom.

Isa the Islamic prophet

People of faith must decide an important question: Will they follow Jesus of Nazareth, or will they follow Muhammad of Mecca? This is a very important choice, with huge consequences for individuals and even for nations.

It is well known that Muslims consider Jesus, whom they call 'Isa', to be a messenger of Allah, just like Muhammad. Islam teaches that Jesus was born miraculously, of the virgin Mary, so he is sometimes referred to as *ibn Maryam* 'son of Mary'. The Quran also calls Isa *al-Masih* 'the Messiah' but no explanation is given about what this title might mean.

Jesus is mentioned in the Quran by the name Isa more than twenty times—in comparison, the name Muhammad is only mentioned four times—and the Quran refers to Jesus by one title or another a total of 93 times.

Islam teaches that before Muhammad there were many messengers or prophets sent by Allah to peoples of the past. The Quran stresses that all these, including Isa, were just human beings.

The Quran claims that these former messengers brought the same message as Muhammad: the message of Islam. For example, it claims that the command to fight and kill and the promise of paradise for believers who die fighting were given to both Jesus and Moses in the past (Q9:111), and later the same command and promise were issued through Muhammad. Of course, the real Jesus of Nazareth did not teach and promise such things.

In the Quran, Isa's disciples declare, "We are Muslims" (Q3:52; see also Q5:111) and the Quran states that Abraham was not a Jew or a Christian but a Muslim (Q3:67). Other biblical figures claimed by the Quran to be prophets of Islam include Abraham, Isaac, Jacob, Ishmael, Moses, Aaron, David, Solomon, Job, Jonah, and John the Baptist.

Islam does allow that the alleged *sharia* brought by these earlier 'prophets of Islam' was not exactly the same as Muhammad's *sharia*. However, it is claimed that the earlier *sharias* were canceled and replaced when Muhammad came, so when Jesus returns he will rule by the *sharia* of Muhammad:

Since the Shari'ah of all the earlier prophets stands abrogated with the advent of Muhammad's apostlehood, Jesus will, therefore, judge according to the law of Islam.[6]

The Quran also claims that Isa was given a book by Allah, called the *Injil*, like Muhammad's Quran. The teaching of the *Injil* is believed to be the same as the message of the Quran, however the original *Injil* text is claimed to be lost. Muslims believe that the Gospels in the Bible contain only changed and corrupted fragments of the original *Injil*. However, it is claimed that this does not matter because Muhammad was sent by Allah to give the final word on what is required.

Essentially, what Islam teaches, and what most Muslims believe, is that if Jesus were alive today he would say to Christians, "Follow Muhammad!" This means that if someone wants to know what Isa actually taught and wants to follow him, what they should do is follow Muhammad and submit to Islam: the Quran explains that a good Christian or a good Jew will recognize Muhammad as a genuine prophet of Allah (Q3:199).

Christians are warned by the Quran not to call Jesus the "Son of God" or to worship him as God. It is stressed that Isa was merely a human being (Q3:59) and a slave of Allah (Q19:30).

Islam teaches that before the world comes to an end, Judaism and Christianity will be destroyed by the hand of Isa. This teaching about the end times helps us understand the Islamic perspective. Consider the following *hadith* from the *Sunan Abu Daud*:

> [When Isa returns] He will fight the people for the cause of Islam. He will break the cross, kill swine, and abolish *jizya*. Allah will cause all religions to perish except Islam. He will destroy the Antichrist and will live on the earth for forty years and then he will die.

Muhammad is saying here that when Isa returns to the earth he will "break the cross"—that is, destroy Christianity—and "abolish *jizya*"—that is, make an end to the legal tolerance of Christians living under Islamic rule. This means that Christians will no longer have the option to pay a tax to keep their Christian religion. Muslim scholars

---

6. *Sahih Muslim*, vol. 2, p. 111, fn. 288.

interpret this to mean that when Isa the Muslim Jesus returns he will compel all non-Muslims, including Christians, to convert to Islam.

Following the real Jesus of Nazareth

We stated earlier that people must decide who they will follow: Jesus or Muhammad. However, Muslims are taught that these are the same choice: to follow Jesus is the same as following Muhammad. Muslims are taught that by following and loving Muhammad, they *are* following Jesus and loving Jesus. Muslims have replaced the Jesus of history, the Jesus of the Gospels, with a different Jesus, Isa of the Quran. This switch of identity conceals God's saving plan and acts as a barrier to Muslims finding and following the true Jesus.

The truth is that the real Jesus of history can be known to us from the four Gospels, which were written down within living memory of Jesus. These are reliable records of Jesus, his message, and his ministry. The teachings of Islam, put together more than 600 years after Jesus walked the earth, cannot be relied upon for information about Jesus of Nazareth.

When someone rejects Islam, they must reject not only the example of Muhammad but also the false Jesus of the Quran. The true and best way to live as a disciple of Jesus is to learn from him and from the message of his followers preserved for us in the four Gospels, as Luke says, "so that you may know the certainty of the things you have been taught" (Luke 1:4).

This is very important because, as we shall see, the key to winning freedom from spiritual bondages is the life and death of Jesus Christ. It is only the true Jesus of Nazareth, the Jesus of the Gospels, who can provide this freedom for us.

Study Guide

Lesson 3

Vocabulary

Islam	messenger	*salat*
shahada	*adhan*	Islamization
Quran	*mushrik*	*Sahih al-Bukhari*
Sunna	*shirk*	*taqiyya*
hadith	People of the Book	*Umma*
sira	*al-Fatihah*	*Injil*

New names

- Amina Lawal: Nigerian woman (born 1972)

- Isa: the Quran's name for Jesus

Bible in this lesson

Luke 1:4

Quran in this lesson

Q33:21	Q8:12-13	Q4:47	Q1:1-7
Q4:80	Q3:85	Q5:15	Q3:28

Q33:36	Q39:65	Q57:28-29	Q9:111
Q24:52	Q9:30-31	Q3:110	Q3:52
Q4:69	Q3:64	Q48:28	Q5:111
Q4:115	Q3:113-14	Q5:72	Q3:67
Q59:7	Q3:199	Q4:47-56	Q3:59
Q9:29	Q98:1	Q5:82	Q19:30

Questions Lesson 3

- Discuss the case study.

How to become a Muslim

1. What is the root meaning and explanation of the Arabic word *Islam*?

2. What do you become if you recite the *shahada*?

3. Who do you declare to become your life guide when you recite the *shahada*?

4. What are the two sources for understanding the guidance from Muhammad, and how do they differ?

5. In which two kinds of texts is the example of Muhammad recorded?

88

Muhammad's personality

6. If Muslims desire to obey Allah, who then must they obey?

7. What are the implications if all of Muhammad's examples are legislated by Allah as the best model for all Muslims to follow?

8. Who are promised to triumph according to Q24:52?

9. What is promised in retribution to those who disobey Allah and his **messenger**?

10. Against whom must Muslims fight, according to Q9:29 and Q8:12-13?

11. Durie notes that Muhammad did some admirable things, yet what eight examples did he list as shocking?

The Quran—Muhammad's personal document

12. If you say the *shahada*, then what are you also obligated to believe in and obey?

13. What illustration does Durie use to explain the relationship between the *Sunna* and the **Quran**?

The Islamic *sharia*—the 'way' to be a Muslim

14. On whom must Muslims rely for expert authority to organize the **Sunna** and the **Quran** into a systematic set of rules, called the *sharia*?

15. According to Durie, without what can there be no Islam?

16. Why is the *sharia* different from laws made by parliaments?

"Come to success"

17. What is the call of Islam?

18. Into which two kinds of people does the **Quran**'s call divide humanity?

19. In what two ways does Islam teach discrimination and feelings of superiority?

A divided world

20. What are the four categories of people in the **Quran** and Islamic law?

21. What does Muhammad call someone who associates anyone or anything with Allah?

22. While Judaism and Christianity (the **People of the Book**) were initially described in the **Quran** to be to be pure forms of monotheism, this changed. Note up to four things for which Muslims now condemn Jews and Christians:

1)

2)

3)

4)

23. What positive things are said of Jews and Christians in the **Quran**?

24. In what way are the four theological claims made by Muslims against non-Muslims also four ways of persecuting Jews and Christians? List all four:

1)

2)

3)

4)

25. How is the relationship of the Jews with Muslims portrayed in the **Quran**?

Jews and Christians in Muslims' daily prayers

26. What three things make the Quran's opening chapter, called **al-Fatihah** 'the Opening' unique?

27. According to Durie, who are the people mentioned in **al-Fatihah** who have gone astray and who are those who have earned Allah's anger?

Problems of the *sharia*

28. What is the fundamental source of problems caused by the *sharia*?

29. What is the name for the process of changing a nation's culture to make it conform to Islam?

30. Identify six problems that Durie attributes to the *sharia:*

   1)

   2)

   3)

   4)

   5)

6)

The case of Amina Lawal

31. What change in Nigeria in 1999 led to **Amina Lawal**'s conviction for adultery?

32. Whose example was the *sharia* judge following closely when he sentenced **Amina Lawal** to be stoned to death?

33. What are Durie's six criticisms of Islam's stoning law?

1)

2)

3)

4)

5)

6)

Lawful deception

34. What several circumstances does Durie cite to illustrate that Muslims may lie?

35. What does *taqiyya* mean?

36. What does Durie see as the ethical damage of habitual lying?

Think for yourself

37. On what do most Muslims rely for guidance in matters of faith?

38. What does Durie encourage us to do now that the primary sources of Islam are available to us in the modern age of the internet?

Isa the Islamic prophet

39. What is the important choice people face?

40. Which name is mentioned more in the **Quran**: Muhammad or Isa (Jesus)?

41. According to Islam, what did Muhammad cause to be abrogated?

42. According to the **Quran**, what was the *Injil*?

43. According to the *hadiths*, what will **Isa** do when he comes back?

Following the real Jesus of Nazareth

44. What are Muslims taught about following Jesus?

45. What does this conceal from Muslims?

46. How can we reliably know about the real Jesus of Nazareth?

47. In what way is it important to distinguish between **Isa** of the **Quran** and Jesus of the Gospels?

4

Muhammad and Rejection

"Love your enemies; do good to those who hate you."
Luke 6:27

Lesson objectives

a. Appreciate the painful first 40 years of Muhammad's life in Arabia.

b. Comprehend how self-rejection and self-doubt in Muhammad were integral to the founding of Islam in Mecca.

c. Grasp how the Meccan 'revelations' were used to validate Muhammad in the face of mockery and persecution from the Meccans.

d. Appreciate the key figures in Muhammad's Meccan life: his ardent supporters and his enraged enemies.

e. Understand how Muhammad's original concept of *fitna* as persecution or temptation was transformed into a violent doctrine of warfare, starting from the late Meccan period and continuing into his years in Medina.

f. Perceive how Muhammad's desire for revenge and vengeance shaped his theology and his treatment of non-believers and especially Jews.

g. Recognize that Muhammad's way to oppose rejection became a global sentiment of victimhood and aggression in Islam.

h. Understand how Muhammad's bad characteristics are reproduced in the lives of Muslims today, due to the influence of the *sharia*.

i. Appreciate the need for those who leave Islam to break away from Muhammad's character and example.

Case study: What would you do?

Your profession requires you to take certain seminars to improve your qualifications. During one workshop, you are placed in a work group where there is a devout Muslim, a cynical atheist, a nominal Catholic, and you. Working with this team sometimes includes eating together. During one mealtime conversation the Muslim gentleman decides to list all the expressions of violence done over the centuries by Christians against Muslims and including all the evil being done against Muslim nations today. As he sees it, "Muslims are oppressed victims; Christians are aggressors." The atheist joins the Muslim in attacking the use of bloody "Holy Wars" by the Crusaders. The Catholic colleague turns red and looks at you for help.

What will you say to both the Muslim and the atheist, who are now also looking at you?

Muhammad is the root and the body of Islam. This lesson gives an overview of some painful experiences in Muhammad's life and the harmful way in which he responded to his difficulties. In the first section we consider his difficult family circumstances and other problems he experienced in Mecca.

Family beginnings

Muhammad was born in c. 570 AD, into the Quraysh, an Arab tribe in Mecca. His father, Abdullah bin Abd al-Muttalib, died before Muhammad was born. Muhammad was then fostered out to another family to be cared for in his early years. His mother died when he was six, and his powerful grandfather looked after him for a while, but then he too passed away when Muhammad was eight. Then Muhammad went to live with his father's brother Abu Talib, where he was given the humble task of looking after his uncle's camels and sheep. Later he claimed that every prophet has shepherded a flock, turning his humble background into something special and distinctive.

Although some of Muhammad's other uncles were wealthy, it seems they did nothing to help him. The Quran expresses contempt for one uncle, nicknamed Abu Lahab or 'father of flame', saying he would burn in hell, because of his contempt for Muhammad:

> Perish the hands of Abu Lahab, and may he perish!
> Neither his wealth nor what he has earned can help him.
> He shall burn in a flaming fire
> and his wife, the carrier of the firewood,
> around her neck a fiber rope. (Q111)

Marriage and family

As a young man, Muhammad was twenty-five and working for a wealthy woman, Khadijah, when she proposed marriage to him. She was older than Muhammad. According to a tradition reported by Ibn Kathir, Khadijah feared that her father would reject the marriage, so she had him marry them while he was drunk. When her father came to his senses he was furious to discover what had happened.

In Arabian culture, a man had to pay a bride price for a wife, after which she was considered his possession. If her husband died, she was even considered part of his estate and his male heir could marry her if he wished. In contrast to the usual situation, Khadijah was powerful and wealthy—Muhammad's biographer Ibn Ishaq called her a woman "of dignity and wealth"—and Muhammad was poor with few prospects. Khadijah had also been married twice before. The contrast between the usual understanding of marriage among Arabs at the time and the arrangement between Khadijah and Muhammad is striking.

Khadijah and Muhammad had six (by some accounts seven) children. All together Muhammad had three (or four) sons, but they all died young, leaving him no male heirs. This was no doubt another source of disappointment in Muhammad's experience of family life, in addition to his childhood experiences.

In conclusion, in Muhammad's family circumstances there were several potentially painful features, including being orphaned and losing his grandfather, becoming a poor dependent relation, having to be married by a drunk father-in-law, loss of his children, and becoming the target of hostility from powerful relatives. The great exceptions to this pattern of rejection and disappointment were the care shown to him by his uncle Abu Talib, and Khadijah's choice of him as a marriage partner, which rescued him from poverty.

A new religion is founded (Mecca)

Muhammad's family circumstances were difficult and when he founded a new religion he continued to experience difficulties.

Muhammad was around 40 years old when he began to experience visitations from a spirit whom he later said was the angel Jibril. At first Muhammad was extremely distressed at these visitations, and wondered whether he was possessed. He even contemplated suicide, saying, "I will go to the top of the mountain and throw myself down that I may kill myself and gain rest." His wife Khadijah comforted him in his great anxiety and took him to her cousin, Waraqa, a Christian, who announced that he was a prophet, and no madman.

Later, when the revelations ceased for a time, Muhammad again had suicidal thoughts, but each time he was about to throw himself off a mountain, Jibril would appear and reassure him, saying, "A new religion Muhammad! You are indeed Allah's messenger in truth."

It seems that Muhammad feared being rejected as a fraud, for in one of the early *suras* Allah assures Muhammad that he would not abandon or reject him (Q93).

The Muslim community grew slowly at first. Khadijah was the first convert. The next was Muhammad's young cousin Ali bin Abu Talib, who had been brought up in Muhammad's own house. Others followed, mainly from among the poor, slaves, and freed slaves.

Muhammad's own tribe

At first the new religion was kept secret by its followers, but after three years Muhammad said Allah had told him to make it public. He did this by convening a family conference at which he invited his relatives into Islam.

At first, Muhammad's fellow Quraysh tribespeople of Mecca were willing to listen to him, but only until he began to attack their gods. After this the Muslims became what Ibn Ishaq called "a despised minority." Tensions ran high, and the two sides came to blows.

As opposition mounted, Muhammad's uncle Abu Talib protected him. When others in Mecca approached saying, "O Abu Talib, your nephew has cursed our gods, insulted our religion, mocked our way of life ... either you must stop him or you must let us get at him," Abu Talib gave them a soft answer and they went away.

The disbelieving Arabs organized an economic and social boycott against Muhammad's clan, forbidding trade and intermarriage with them. Because of their poverty, the Muslims were vulnerable. Ibn Ishaq summarizes their treatment at the hands of the Quraysh:

> Then the Quraysh showed their enmity to all those who
> followed the apostle; every clan which contained Muslims
> attacked them [the Muslims], imprisoning them, and beating
> them, allowing them no food or drink, and exposing them to the
> burning heat of Mecca, so as to seduce them from their religion.
> Some gave way under pressure of persecution, and others
> resisted them, being protected by God.[7]

Muhammad himself did not escape the dangers and insults: he had dirt and even animal intestines thrown over him when he was praying.

When the persecution continued, 83 Muslim men and their families emigrated to Christian Abyssinia for refuge, where they found protection.

In these next sections we consider how Muhammad responded to rejection by his own people in Mecca.

Self-doubt and self-validation

At one point Muhammad appeared to waver in his belief in one god under pressure from the Quraysh. They had offered a deal to him whereby they would worship Allah if he worshipped their gods. He would not accept this deal, announcing the verses of Q109:6, "To you your religion, to me my religion!" However, Muhammad must have hesitated, for al-Tabari records that as he was receiving Q53, there

---

7. A. Guillaume, *The Life of Muhammad*, p. 143.

were "revealed" to him what came to be known as the 'Satanic Verses', which said of the Meccan goddesses al-Lat, al-Uzza, and Manat, "These are the exalted *gharaniq* (cranes) whose intercession is approved."

When they heard this verse, the heathen Quraysh were delighted and began to worship with the Muslims. However, the angel Jibril rebuked Muhammad, so Muhammad announced that the verse was abrogated (canceled) and had come from Satan. When Muhammad made it known that the verse had been withdrawn, this attracted more scorn from the Quraysh, who became even more hostile to Muhammad and his followers.

After this, Muhammad reported a verse that claimed that all prophets before him had also been led astray by Satan (Q22:52). Here again we see Muhammad taking a potential cause for shame and turning it into a mark of distinction.

In the face of mockery and charges that he was a faker, which stung him deeply, Muhammad reported receiving verses from Allah that validated him, and praised his character for being remarkable. He was not in error, the Quran states, but a man of integrity (Q53:1-3; Q68:1-4).

A variety of *hadith* traditions also report that Muhammad came to believe in the superiority of his race, tribe, clan, and parentage. In response to claims that he was illegitimate, he said that all his ancestors were born in, and none out of, wedlock, all the way back to Adam. In a *hadith* reported by Ibn Kathir, Muhammad announced that he was the best man from the best clan (the Hashemites) of the best nation (the Arabs), saying, "I am the best of you in spirit and the best of you in parentage ... I am the choicest of the chosen; so whoever loves the Arabs, it is through loving me that he loves them."

It was during Muhammad's 13 years in Mecca that the Islamic concept of success and the language of winners and losers began to emerge as themes in the Quran. For example, in repeated references to the conflicts between Moses and the Egyptian idolaters, the Quran describes the outcomes in terms of winners and losers (for example, Q20:64, 68; Q26:40-44). Muhammad also began to apply the terminology of success to the struggle between himself and his opponents, declaring that those who reject Allah's revelations will be losers (Q10:95).

More rejection and new allies

Things had not been going well for some time in Mecca when Muhammad lost both his wife Khadijah and his uncle Abu Talib in the same year. These were huge blows. Without their support and protection, the Quraysh were made bold to be even more hostile against Muhammad and his religion.

Arab society was based on alliances and client relationships. The way to find security was to come under the protection of someone more powerful than oneself. With dangers to him and his followers increasing, and having been rejected by his own tribe, Muhammad went to Ta'if, a place near Mecca, to seek alternative protectors. However, at Ta'if he was mocked and ridiculed and was chased away by a mob.

On the way back from Ta'if, Islamic tradition reports that a group of *jinn* (demons) heard Muhammad reciting verses from the Quran while saying his prayers in the middle of the night. They were so impressed at what they heard that they accepted Islam straight away. Then these Muslim demons went off to preach Islam to other *jinn*. This incident is referred to twice in the Quran (Q46:29-32; Q72:1-15).

This incident is important for two reasons. First, it is consistent with Muhammad's pattern of self-validation: he was able to claim that even though the humans at Ta'if had rejected him, there were *jinn* who recognized him for what he claimed to be: a genuine messenger from Allah.

Second, the idea that *jinn* can be god-fearing Muslims opened a doorway within Islam to the demonic realm. This incident in Muhammad's life, and its reference to Muslim *jinn*, has provided a justification for Muslims to try to make contact with the (Muslim) spirit world. Another reason for Muslims to engage with the spirit world is the references in the Quran and the *hadiths* to each person having a *qarin* or companion spirit (Q43:36; Q50:23, 27).

Back in Mecca, things were not looking good for Muhammad. Yet eventually he did manage to find a community that was willing to protect him. These were Arabs from Yathrib (later called Medina), a city where many Jews also lived. During an annual fair in Mecca, a group of visitors from Medina pledged loyalty and obedience to Muhammad, agreeing to live by his message of monotheism.

In this first pledge, no commitment to fight was made. However, at the next year's fair a larger group of Medinans pledged the protection that Muhammad had been seeking. These Medinans, who came to be known as the *Ansar* 'helpers', undertook to wage "war in complete obedience to the apostle."

After this it was decided that the Meccan Muslims would emigrate to Medina to form a political safe haven. Muhammad was the last to flee Mecca, escaping in the middle of the night through a back window. In Medina, Muhammad was able to proclaim his message unhindered, and virtually all the Medinan Arabs converted to Islam within the first year. Muhammad was by this time just over 52 years old.

During the Meccan years, Muhammad had been rejected by his own family and tribe. With few exceptions, only the humble poor had believed in him, and he had been mocked, threatened, humiliated, and attacked by all the rest.

Muhammad had been very unsure of himself at first, fearing rejection of his sense of prophetic calling. At one point he even seemed to accept the Quraysh's gods. However, in the end, despite all the opposition, Muhammad acted with determined perseverance and acquired a group of dedicated followers.

Was Muhammad really peaceful in Mecca?

Many writers have claimed that Muhammad's decade of witness in Mecca was peaceful. In one sense this was true. However, although no physical violence is commanded in the Meccan chapters of the Quran, it was certainly contemplated, and the early revelations denounce Muhammad's neighbors in terrifying language, announcing terrible torments in the next life for those who reject his religion.

One of the functions of the Meccan judgment verses in the Quran was to validate Muhammad in the face of rejection from the Quraysh

Arabs. For example, the Quran says that those who laugh at the Muslims will be punished in this life and the next. The believers, sitting back drinking wine in luxury on their couches in paradise, will laugh when they gaze down at the unbelievers roasting in hellfire (Q83:29-36).

These judgment messages undoubtedly stoked the fires of conflict in Mecca. The disbelieving idolaters did not like what they were hearing.

Not only did Muhammad preach eternal judgment, but Ibn Ishaq reports that it was early in the Meccan period that Muhammad first foreshadowed his intention to kill the disbelieving Meccans. He said to them, "Will you listen to me, O Quraysh? By him who holds my life in his hand, I bring you slaughter."

Later, just before Muhammad fled to Medina, a group of Quraysh came to him and confronted him with the charge that he was threatening to kill those who rejected him: "Muhammad alleges that … if you do not follow him you will be slaughtered, and when you are raised from the dead you will be burned in the fire of hell." Muhammad confessed this was correct, saying, "I do say that."

After suffering rejection and persecution in Mecca, the Muslim community, guided by their prophet Muhammad, chose to go to war against their opponents.

In these sections we examine Muhammad's turn to violence against those who rejected him and his message.

From persecution to killing

The Arabic word *fitna* 'trial, persecution, temptation' is crucial for understanding Muhammad's metamorphosis into a military leader. The word is derived from *fatana* 'to turn away from, to tempt, seduce, or subject to trials'. Its base meaning is to test and purify a metal with fire. *Fitna* can refer to either temptation or trial, including both positive and negative means of persuasion. It could include offering financial and other incentives or applying torture.

Fitna became a key concept in theological reflection upon the early Muslim community's experiences with unbelievers. Muhammad's charge against the Quraysh was that they used *fitna*—including insult, slander, torture, exclusion, economic pressures, and other incentives—in order to get Muslims to leave Islam or to dilute its claims.

The earliest quranic verses concerning fighting made clear that the whole purpose of fighting and killing was to eliminate *fitna*:

> Fight in the way of Allah against those who fight against you,
> but do not commit aggression: Allah does not love aggressors.
> Kill them wherever you come upon them,
> and expel them from where they expelled you.
> Persecution [*fitna*] is worse than killing.
> ....
>
> Fight them until there is no persecution [*fitna*]
> and the religion is Allah's.
> But if they stop [cease their disbelief and opposition to Islam],
> there shall be no aggression except against evildoers.
> (Q2:190-93)

The idea that *fitna* of Muslims was "worse than killing" proved to be very significant. The same phrase would be revealed again after an attack on a Meccan caravan (Q2:217) during the sacred month (a period during which Arab tribal traditions prohibited raiding). It implied, at the very least, that shedding the blood of infidels is not as bad as leading Muslims astray from their faith.

Another significant phrase in this passage from Sura 2 is "fight them until there is no *fitna*." This too was revealed a second time, after the Battle of Badr, during the second year in Medina (Q8:39).

These *fitna* phrases, each revealed twice, established the principle that *jihad* was justified by the existence of any obstacle to people entering Islam, or of incentives to Muslims to abandon their faith. However grievous it might be to fight and kill others, undermining or obstructing Islam was worse.

Muslim scholars extended the concept of *fitna* to include even the mere existence of unbelief, so the phrase could be interpreted as "unbelief is worse than killing."

Understood this way, the phrase "*fitna* is worse than killing" became a universal mandate to fight and kill all infidels who rejected

Muhammad's message, whether they were interfering with Muslims or not. For unbelievers to merely "commit disbelief"—as the great commentator Ibn Kathir put it—was a greater evil than their being killed. This provided the justification for warfare to eliminate disbelief, and make Islam dominant over all other religions (Q2:193; Q8:39).

"We are the victims!"

Through these passages in the Quran, Muhammad was emphasizing the victimhood of Muslims. To make fighting and conquest appear righteous he claimed that infidel enemies were guilty and deserved to be attacked. The greater victimhood of Muslims was used to justify the violence: the more extreme the punishment inflicted by Muslims on their enemies, the more necessary it was to insist upon the enemies' guilt. After Allah declared that Muslims' sufferings were "worse than killing," it became obligatory for Muslims to regard their own victimhood as a greater evil than whatever they inflicted upon their enemies.

It is this theological root, grounded in the Quran and the *Sunna* of Muhammad, that explains why, again and again, some Muslims have insisted that their victimhood is greater than that of those they have attacked. This mentality was displayed by Ahmad bin Muhammad, Algerian Professor of Religious Politics, in a debate with Dr Wafa Sultan on Al-Jazeera television. Dr Sultan had pointed out that Muslims had killed innocent people. Infuriated by Dr Sultan's arguments, Ahmad bin Muhammad began shouting:

> We are the victims! ... There are millions of innocent people among us [Muslims], while the innocent among you ... number only dozens, hundreds, or thousands, at the most.

This victim mentality continues to plague many Muslim communities to this day, and weakens their capacity to take responsibility for their own actions.

Retribution

As Muhammad's military strength in Medina grew and victories began to come, his treatment of defeated enemies revealed a lot about his motivations for fighting. A telling incident was Muhammad's treatment of Uqba, who had earlier thrown camel dung and intestines on him. Uqba was captured in the Battle of Badr, and pleaded for his life, saying, "But who will look after my children, O Muhammad?" The answer was "Hell!" Then Muhammad had Uqba killed. After the battle of Badr, the bodies of the Meccans killed in the fighting were thrown into a pit and Muhammad went to the pit in the middle of the night to mock the Meccan dead.

Such incidents show that Muhammad sought to validate himself by taking revenge against those who had rejected him. He insisted on having the last word, even to the dead.

Those who rejected Muhammad were at the top of his assassination list. When he conquered Mecca, Muhammad discouraged killing. However, there was a small hit list of people to be killed. This list included three apostates, a man and a woman who had insulted Muhammad in Mecca, and two slave girls who used to sing satirical songs about him.

The Meccan hit list reflects Muhammad's revulsion at being rejected. The apostates' continued existence was a form of *fitna*, for as long as they lived they were proof that it was possible to leave Islam, while those who mocked or insulted Muhammad were dangerous because they had the power to undermine the faith of others.

Implications for non-Muslims

The root of the rejection of non-believers in Islamic law is found in Muhammad's emotional worldview and his own responses to rejection.

Initially, Muhammad focused his enmity on his fellow tribespeople, the pagan Arabs. We can observe a trend in Muhammad's treatment of the pagan Arabs: a sense of offense at the trials they heaped upon the Muslims is used to justify the idea that the very existence of disbelief constitutes *fitna*. The same trend also is found in Muhammad's dealings with the People of the Book. As rejectors of Islam, they became permanently marked as guilty, deserving to be dominated, and treated as inferior.

Before the conquest of Mecca, Muhammad had a vision in which he performed a pilgrimage to Mecca. This was impossible at the time, as the Muslims were in a state of war with the Meccans. After his vision, Muhammad negotiated the Treaty of Hudaybiyyah, which allowed him to make his pilgrimage. The treaty was to be for ten years, and one of its stipulations was that Muhammad would return to the Meccans anyone who came to him without the permission of their guardian. This included slaves and women. The treaty also allowed people from either side to enter into alliances with each other.

Muhammad did not keep his side of the treaty: when people came to him from Mecca to reclaim their wives or slaves he would refuse to return the fugitives, citing the authority of Allah. The first case was a woman, Umm Kulthum, whose brothers came to retrieve her. Muhammad refused, for, as Ibn Ishaq put it, "Allah forbade it" (see also Q60:10).

Sura 60 instructs the Muslims not to take unbelievers as their friends. It says that if any Muslims secretly love the Meccans they have gone astray, since the unbelievers' desire is only to cause the Muslims to disbelieve. The whole of Sura 60 is in conflict with the spirit of the Treaty of Hudaybiyyah, which had stated, "We will not show enmity one to another and there shall be no secret reservation or bad faith." However, later, when the Muslims attacked and conquered Mecca, this was said to be justified on the basis that it was the Quraysh who violated the treaty.

After this, Allah declared that no more treaties could be made with idolaters—"Allah renounces the idolators" and "kill the idolaters wherever you find them" (Q9:3, 5).

This sequence of events illustrates what became an established Islamic view, that non-Muslim disbelievers were by nature pact breakers, unable to keep covenants (Q9:7-8). At the same time, Muhammad, under instruction from Allah, claimed his right to break pacts with infidels. When Muhammad, claiming the authority of a higher power, violated his agreements, this was not regarded as unrighteous.

Incidents like these reveal that Muhammad, by consigning unbelievers to the category of those who would seduce Muslims from their faith (i.e. those who would commit *fitna*), made it impossible to have normal relationships with them as long as they refused to accept Islam.

In these next sections we consider how Muhammad turned his resentment and aggression against the Jews of Arabia, with tragic consequences. Muhammad's interactions with the Jews of Arabia form the foundation of Islam's policy on non-Muslims, including the *dhimma* covenant system for People of the Book, which we will explore in a later lesson.

Muhammad's early views on the Jews

At first Muhammad's main interest in Jews concerned his claim that he was a prophet in a long line that included many Jewish prophets. In the late Meccan and early Medinan period, there are numerous references to Jews, often referring to them as People of the Book. During this time the Quran makes the point that although some Jews were believing and some were not, Muhammad's message would come as a blessing to them (Q98:1-8).

Muhammad had also encountered some Christians, and these contacts had been encouraging. Khadijah's Christian cousin Waraqa had identified Muhammad as a prophet. There is also a tradition that on his travels Muhammad met a monk called Bahira, who declared that Muhammad was a prophet. Perhaps Muhammad hoped that Jews would see in him a "clear sign" from Allah (Q98) and respond positively to his message. Indeed, Muhammad said that what he was teaching was the same as the Jewish religion, including "performing the prayer" and paying *zakat*[8] (Q98:5). He even directed his followers to pray facing *al-Sham* 'Syria', which is interpreted to mean toward Jerusalem, copying the Jewish custom.

When Muhammad arrived in Medina, Islamic tradition records that he implemented a covenant between Muslims and Jews. This covenant recognized the Jewish religion—"the Jews have their religion and the Muslims have theirs"—and it commanded loyalty from the Jews to Muhammad.

---

8. One of the five pillars of Islam, *zakat* is an annual religious tax.

Opposition in Medina

Muhammad began to present his message to the Jewish residents of Medina, but met with unexpected resistance. Islamic tradition attributes this to envy. Some of Muhammad's revelations included biblical references, and no doubt the rabbis contested this material, pointing out contradictions in Muhammad's interpretations.

The prophet of Islam found the rabbis' questions troublesome, and at times more of the Quran would be sent down to him, supplying him with replies. Again and again, when Muhammad was challenged by a question, he would turn the incident into an opportunity for self-validation, as the verses of the Quran show.

One of Muhammad's simplest strategies was to assert that the Jews were deceivers who quoted passages that suited them while concealing others that would not help their cause (Q36:76; Q2:77). Another answer from Allah was that the Jews had deliberately falsified their scriptures (Q2:75).

The rabbis' conversations with Muhammad were interpreted by Islamic tradition not as genuine dialogue or reasonable answers to Muhammad's claims, but as *fitna*, an attempt to destroy Islam and the faith of Muslims.

A hostile theology of rejectors

Muhammad's frustrating conversations with Jews contributed to his growing hostility to them. Whereas in the past, verses of the Quran had said that some Jews were believers, later the Quran declared that the whole Jewish race was cursed and only very few were true believers (Q4:46).

The Quran claimed that in the past some Jews were transformed into monkeys and pigs for their sins (Q2:65; Q5:60; Q7:166). Allah also called them prophet-killers (Q4:155; Q5:70). Allah was said to have renounced his relationship with the covenant-breaking Jews, hardening their hearts, therefore Muslims could always expect to find them treacherous (except for a few) (Q5:13). Having broken their covenant, the Jews were declared to be "losers" who had forsaken their true guidance (Q2:27).

In Medina, Muhammad came to the view that he had been sent to correct the errors of the Jews (Q5:15). Early in the Medinan period, Muhammad's revelations had suggested that Judaism was valid (Q2:62). However, this verse was abrogated by Q3:85. Muhammad concluded that his coming had abrogated Judaism, that the Islam he brought was the final religion, and that the Quran was the last revelation. All who rejected this message would be "losers" (Q3:85). It would no longer be acceptable for Jews—or Christians—to follow their old religion: they had to acknowledge Muhammad, and become Muslims too.

In the verses of the Quran, Muhammad launched a full-scale theological attack on Judaism. This arose out of the profound offense taken by Muhammad at the Jews' rejection of his message. This was another self-validation for Muhammad, like those he had resorted to with the Meccan idolaters. Then Muhammad went further, and implemented aggressive responses as well.

Rejection turns into violence

In Medina, Muhammad began a campaign to intimidate and ultimately to eliminate the Jews. Emboldened by victory over the idolaters at the Battle of Badr, he visited the Qaynuqa' Jewish tribe and threatened them with God's vengeance. Then he found an excuse to besiege the Qaynuqa' Jews and expelled them from Medina.

Then Muhammad commenced a series of targeted assassinations of Jews, and issued a command to his followers, "Kill any Jew that falls into your power." To the Jews he announced *aslim taslam* 'accept Islam and you will be safe'.

A profound shift had taken place in Muhammad's understanding. Non-Muslims had rights to their property and lives only if they had supported and honored Islam and Muslims. Anything else was *fitna*, and an excuse for fighting them.

Muhammad's task of dealing with the Jews of Medina was not yet complete. The Banu Nadir were next in line to come under his attention. The whole Nadir tribe was accused of breaking their covenant, so they were attacked and, after an extended siege, were likewise driven out of Medina, abandoning their property as booty for the Muslims.

After this Muhammad besieged the last remaining Jewish tribe, the Banu Qurayza, on the basis of a command from the angel Jibril. When the Jews surrendered unconditionally, the Jewish men were beheaded in the marketplace of Medina—600 to 900 hundred men, by various accounts—and the Jewish women and children were distributed as booty (i.e. as slaves) among the Muslims.

Muhammad was not quite finished with the Jews of Arabia. After clearing Medina of their presence he attacked Khaybar. The Khaybar campaign started out with a two-choice offer to the Jews: convert to Islam or be killed. However, when the Muslims defeated the Jews of Khaybar, a third choice was negotiated: conditional surrender. This is how the Khaybar Jews become the first *dhimmis* (see Lesson 6).

This concludes our discussion of Muhammad's dealings with the Jews.

It is important to note that since the Quran treats Christians and Jews alike as representatives of a single category known as the People of the Book, the treatment of Jews in the Quran and in the life of Muhammad, as People of the Book, became a model for the treatment of Christians down through the ages as well.

Muhammad's three responses to rejection

In the story of Muhammad's prophetic career we have seen how he experienced rejection in many ways: in his family circumstances, by his own community in Mecca, and by the Jews in Medina.

We also have also observed a range of his responses to rejection. Early on, Muhammad showed *self-rejecting responses*, including suicidal thoughts, fear that he was possessed, and despair.

There were also *self-validating responses*, as if to counter the fear of rejection. [9] These include assertions that Allah would punish his enemies in hell; claims to cover points of potential embarrassment, such as the assertion that all prophets had been led astray at some point by Satan; and verses sent down from Allah that declared that

---

9. For a discussion of rejection and responses to it, see Noel and Phyl Gibson, *Evicting Demonic Squatters and Breaking Bondages*.

those who followed Muhammad's revelations would be winners in this life and the next.

Finally, *aggressive responses* came to dominate. These resulted in the doctrine of *jihad* to eliminate *fitna* by fighting against and conquering non-Muslims.

In his responses, Muhammad passed through self-rejection, then self-validation, and finally aggression. Muhammad the orphan became Muhammad the orphan-maker. The self-doubter, who had contemplated suicide because he feared he was being tormented by demons, became the ultimate rejector, imposing his creed through fighting to supersede and ultimately replace all other faiths.

In Muhammad's emotional worldview, the defeat and degradation of disbelievers would "heal" his followers' feelings and quench their rage. This healing 'Islamic peace', won through battle, is described in the Quran:

> Fight them! Allah will punish them by your hands and disgrace them, and help you against them, heal the hearts of a people who believe, and take away rage from their hearts. (Q9:14-15)

At first, Muhammad and his followers did experience actual persecution at the hands of the Meccan polytheists. However, when he took power in Medina, Muhammad came to regard even disbelief in his prophethood as persecution of Muslims, and licensed the use of violence to deal with disbelievers and mockers—whether idolators, Jews, or Christians—so they would be silenced and intimidated into submission. Muhammad established an ideological and military program to eliminate all forms of rejection of him, his religion, and his community. Later he claimed that the success of his program validated and vindicated his prophethood.

At the same time that all this was happening, Muhammad was exerting more and more control over his followers, the Muslims. Whereas earlier in Mecca the Quran had declared that Muhammad was "just a warner," after the migration to Medina he became a commander of the faithful, regulating their lives to the point where the Quran declares that once "Allah and the messenger" have decided a matter, there is nothing left for believers but to obey without question (Q33:36), and the way to obey Allah is to obey the messenger (Q4:80).

The controls Muhammad introduced in the Medinan period continue to cause trauma for many Muslims today through the *sharia*. One example is a law of the *sharia*, introduced by Muhammad, that if a man divorces his wife by saying, "I divorce you" three times, but after that the couple wants to remarry, she must first marry another man, have sex with him, and be divorced by her second husband before she can remarry her first husband. This rule has caused a lot of grief to Muslim women.

The Quran shows us the progress of Muhammad's prophetic career: it is Muhammad's own, intensely personal document, a record of his growing sense of hostility and aggression in the face of rejection, and of his growing willingness to control the lives of others. The characteristics that later came to be imposed upon non-Muslims—such as silence, guilt, and gratitude—came from the evolution of Muhammad's own responses to rejection, as he violently forced failure and rejection upon all who refused to declare, "I believe there is no god but Allah and Muhammad is his prophet."

This concludes our overview of Muhammad's experience of and responses to rejection, both received and imposed upon others, and his self-validating pursuit of success over his enemies.

The "best example"

In this lesson we have been learning about some of the key characteristics of Muhammad. Although he is considered in Islam to be the best example for humanity to follow, we have seen that he was impacted and indeed deeply damaged by rejection. His responses included self-rejection, self-validation, control, and aggression. These responses to rejection were harmful to him and continue to be harmful to many other people to this day.

Muhammad's personal history is important because his personal problems have become world problems though the *sharia* and its worldview. In this way a Muslim is bound spiritually to the character and example of Muhammad. This bond is asserted through the ritual of reciting the *shahada*, and it is reinforced through the rituals of Islam whenever the *shahada* is recited. The first words a Muslim baby hears after it is born is the declaration of the *shahada* recited into its ears.

116

The *shahada* declares that Muhammad is Allah's messenger, which is an endorsement of the Quran as the word of Allah, sent down to Muhammad as Allah's messenger. To affirm the *shahada* gives consent to what the Quran says about Muhammad, including the obligation to follow his example, the acceptance of threats and curses that Muhammad pronounced on those who do not follow him, and the duty to oppose and even fight against those who reject his message and refuse to follow him.

In effect, the *shahada* is a declaration to the spirit world—to the authorities and powers of this dark world (Ephesians 6:12)—that the believer is bound by a covenant to conform to Muhammad's example: he or she has a 'soul tie' to Muhammad (see Lesson 7). This establishes a spiritual bond with Muhammad. This covenant bond gives permission to the authorities and powers to impose upon Muslim believers the same moral and spiritual problems that challenged and bound Muhammad, and which have become embedded in and reinforced through the Islamic *sharia*, working their way deep into the cultures of Islamic societies.

We have been discussing just some of the many negative aspects of Muhammad's *Sunna* which are replicated through the lives of many Muslims due to the influence of the *shahada* and the *sharia*. Here is a list of some of the negative characteristics which characterized Muhammad's example and teaching:

- violence and warfare
- murder
- slavery
- retaliation and revenge
- hatred
- hatred of women
- hatred of Jews
- abuse
- shame and shaming of others
- intimidation

- deception
- taking offense
- victimhood
- self-vindication
- feelings of superiority
- misrepresenting God
- dominating others
- rape.

When Muslims recite the *shahada* they are in effect endorsing the Quran's and *Sunna's* claims about Christ and the Bible. These include:

- denial of Christ's death on the cross
- hatred of the cross
- denial that Jesus is the Son of God (and curses upon those who believe this)
- the accusation that Jews and Christians have corrupted their scriptures
- the claim that Jesus will return to destroy Christianity and force the whole world to submit to Muhammad's *sharia*.

These attributes are a heavy burden indeed. One of the challenges faced by those who leave Islam to follow Jesus Christ is that unless these characteristics are dealt with decisively they will continue to find a foothold in people's souls. This is one reason why Muslims who turn to Christ can experience struggles and difficulties in their Christian walk.

If the status of Muhammad as a messenger is not explicitly renounced, then the curses and threats of the Quran and Muhammad's opposition to the death of Christ and the lordship of Christ can be a cause of spiritual instability, causing someone to be easily intimidated, and breeding vulnerability and a lack of confidence as a follower of Jesus. This can severely damage someone's discipleship.

Because of this, when someone leaves Islam, it is recommended that they should specifically reject and renounce the example and teaching of Muhammad, as well as the Quran, together with the legacy and all the curses implied by the *shahada*. We will learn how to do this in the next lesson as we consider the life of Jesus Christ and his cross, and propose powerful keys to be set free from the example of Muhammad.

Study Guide

Lesson 4

Vocabulary

Satanic Verses	Treaty of Hudaybiyyah
abrogation	*zakat*
jinn	*aslim taslam*
qarin	*Khaybar*
migration	*dhimmi*
fitna	People of the Book

Rejection reactions: self-rejection, self-validation, aggression

New names

- The Quraysh, Muhammad's tribe in Mecca
- Abdullah bin Abd al-Muttalib: Muhammad's Arab father (died 570 AD)
- Abu Talib: Muhammad's uncle and patron (died 620 AD)
- Abu Lahab: Muhammad's uncle and opponent (died 624 AD)
- Khadijah: Muhammad's Meccan wife (died 620 AD)
- Ibn Kathir: Syrian historian and scholar (1301-1373 AD)
- Ibn Ishaq: Syrian Muslim biographer of Muhammad (704-768 AD). His account of Muhammad's life was recorded—in edited form—by Ibn Hisham (c. 833 AD).
- Jibril: an alleged angel who sent messages to Muhammad
- Waraqa: the Christian cousin of Khadijah, Muhammad's first wife

- Ali bin Abu Talib: Muhammad's younger cousin, son of Abu Talib and Muhammad's second convert (601-661 AD)
- Al-Tabari: an influential Muslim historian and commentator on the Quran (839-923 AD)
- Al-Lat, al-Uzza, and Manat: Meccan goddesses, the three daughters of Allah
- Hashemites: descendants of Muhammad's great grandfather, Hashim
- Yathrib: an earlier name for Medina
- The Ansar 'helpers': Medinans who followed Muhammad
- Dr Wafa Sultan: Syrian-American psychiatrist and critic of Islam (born 1958 AD)
- Ahmad bin Muhammad: Algerian Professor of Religious Politics
- Uqba: a Meccan Arab hostile to Muhammad
- Bahira: a Christian monk whom Muhammad met on his travels
- Banu Qaynuqaʿ, Banu Nadir and Banu Qurayza: Medinan Jewish tribes

Bible in this lesson

Ephesians 6:12

Quran in this lesson

Q111	Q46:29-32	Q36:76	Q2:27
Q93	Q71:1-15	Q2:77	Q5:15
Q109:6	Q83:29-36	Q2:75	Q2:62
Q53	Q2:190-93	Q4:46	Q3:85
Q22:52	Q2:217	Q2:65	Q9:14-15
Q53:1-3	Q8:39	Q5:60	Q33:36
Q68:1-4	Q2:193	Q7:166	Q4:80

Q20:64, 69   Q60:10   Q4:155

Q26:40-44   Q9:3-5, 7-8   Q5:70

Q10:95   Q98:1-8   Q5:13

Questions Lesson 4

- Discuss the case study.

Family beginnings

1. What three painful events happened during the early years of Muhammad?

2. For what is Muhammad's uncle **Abu Lahab** known?

3. What are six unique aspects of Muhammad's marriage to **Khadijah**?

4. What suffering did Muhammad and **Khadijah** encounter in childbearing?

5. Who were the two figures who showed great care to Muhammad?

A new religion is founded (Mecca)

6. How old was Muhammad when he began to experience visitations from the 'angel' **Jibril** and how did he respond to them?

7. When **Waraqa** heard of Muhammad's visitations, what did he announce?

8. What did Muhammad repeatedly fear, which Allah repeatedly assured him he was not?

9. Who were the first Muslim believers?

Muhammad's own tribe

10. What caused Muhammad's small community of Muslims to become a despised minority?

11. What important role did Uncle **Abu Talib** have, even though he was not a Muslim?

12. What became the new policy of the **Quraysh** tribe in Mecca toward Muhammad and his community?

13. To which Christian nation did many Muslims flee and how many men fled with their families?

Self-doubt and self-validation

14. What deal was Muhammad offered to which Q109:6 was addressed?

15. What concession did Muhammad make that made the Meccans rejoice but which he later reversed, and which is now called the **Satanic Verses?**

16. Following Muhammad's reversal, what excuse did Q22:52 make?

17. What numerous boasts did Muhammad make to promote his superiority?

18. What became Muhammad's new concept of 'success' at the end of the Meccan period?

More rejection and new allies

19. What double blow awaited Muhammad and where did he find new protectors?

20. When Muhammad was returning from Ta'if, who became Muslims when they heard him praying?

21. What two reasons does Durie give for the openness of many Muslims to the spirit world?

22. What is the pledge the **Ansar** from Medina made to Muhammad?

23. What did Muhammad achieve in his first year in Medina which he did not achieve in Mecca?

Was Muhammad Really Peaceful in Mecca?

24. What dire announcements are found in the Meccan Suras?

25. What, according to **Ibn Ishaq**, did Muhammad promise would happen to the Meccan **Quraysh** tribe?

From persecution to killing

26. What did Muhammad accuse the **Quraysh** of using against him which, in turn, justified the whole purpose of fighting?

27. According to Muhammad, what is more grievous than killing people or violently violating the sacred month?

28. What always justifies *jihad*?

29. If you 'commit disbelief', what do you deserve, according to Muslim scholars and the Syrian Persian scholar **Ibn Kathir**?

"We are the victims!"

30. Why do Muslims regard their victimhood as worse than their killing of their enemies?

31. On what did Professor **Ahmad bin Muhammad** base his case for victimhood when debating Dr **Wafa Sultan**?

Retribution

32. What does Muhammad's treatment of **Uqba** and his behavior indicate?

33. What does Muhammad's assassination hit list of captured Meccans reflect?

Implications for non-Muslims

34. What awaited the **People of the Book** when they too rejected Islam?

35. What, according to Durie, came to dominate in Muhammad's life?

36. Why did Muhammad feel he could violate the **Treaty of Hudaybiyyah**?

37. What does Q9:3-5 instruct Muslims to do with idolaters?

Muhammad's early views on the Jews

38. How are the Jews spoken of in the Quran's
    Meccan Suras and in Sura 98?

39. What indicates that Muhammad had hoped
    that the Jews would respond positively to
    his message?

Opposition in Medina

40. Why did Muhammad have to rely increasingly on newer
    quranic revelations in his exchanges with Medina's Jewish
    rabbis?

41. In what two ways did Muhammad respond to the *fitna* of the
    Jews?

A hostile theology of rejectors

42. Durie describes Muhammad's new anti-Jewish message: what
    does the Quran say what "Jews were"?

    1) Q4:46 …

    2) Q7:166, etc …

    3) Q5:70 …

    4) Q5:13 …

5) Q2:27 ...

43. What did Muhammad now believe his message had **abrogated**?

Rejection turns into violence

44. What did Muhammad do to the first Medinan Jewish **Qaynuqa'** tribe?

45. Why did Muhammad preach *aslim taslam* to the remaining Jews in Medina?

46. What did Muhammad do to the second Medinan Jewish **Nadir** tribe?

47. What did Muhammad do to the third Medinan Jewish **Qurayza** tribe?

48. What did Muhammad do to the **Khaybar** Jewish tribe?

49. Who are viewed as the **People of the Book** in Islam?

Muhammad's three responses to rejection

50. As a result of multiple forms of **rejection**, through what three stages did Muhammad pass in response?

51. According to Q9:14-15, what would "heal" Muhammad and his followers' sentiments and quench their rage?

52. What did Muhammad do to stop rejection of him and his community?

53. What was the change in Muhammad's role after migration to Medina?

54. What do later verses in the Quran consider to be the way to obey Allah?

55. On what are the mandatory silence, guilt, and gratitude of non-Muslims based?

The "best example"

56. How have Muhammad's problems become problems for the world?

57. What are the first words recited into a newborn Muslim baby's ear?

58. What two things do Muslims endorse when they say the *shahada*?

59. According to Durie, what permission does reciting the *shahada* give to the spiritual powers?

60. If you have personally encountered Muslims, have you observed in their conduct any of the 18 aspects of Muhammad's example listed below? (Circle one or more.)

- violence / warfare
- murder
- slavery
- retaliation / revenge
- hatred
- hatred of women
- hatred of Jews
- abuse
- shame / shaming
- intimidation

- deception
- taking offense
- victimhood
- self-validation
- feelings of superiority
- misrepresenting God
- dominating others
- rape
- none of the above

61. How do the Quran and the *Sunna* react to Christ's divine Sonship?

62. How do the Quran and the *Sunna* react to the Bible?

63. What do the Quran and the *Sunna* say that Jesus (Isa) will do to Christians when he returns to earth?

64. When we reject and renounce the example of Muhammad and accompanying curses, what else do we reject?

65. What four spiritual characteristics can result from the failure to explicitly renounce Muhammad?

5

Freedom from the *Shahada*

"If anyone is in Christ, that person is a new creation."
2 Corinthians 5:17

Lesson objectives

a. Contrast and understand how different Jesus and Muhammad were in the way they responded to rejection.

b. Survey the many ways in which Jesus was questioned, rejected, and despised.

c. Understand how Jesus embraced rejection and rejected violence.

d. Appreciate the profound impact of Christ's teaching of loving our enemies.

e. Accept that Jesus prepared his disciples and all Christians for eventual persecution.

f. Grasp how God addresses human and divine rejection in the death of Jesus Christ on the cross.

g. Comprehend how the resurrection and ascension display the vindication of Jesus Christ's death.

h. Be aware of the intense hatred Muhammad had for the cross of Jesus.

i. Establish a commitment to Christ by reciting a prayer to follow him.

j. Consider scriptural verses declaring 15 specific truths as you prepare to renounce the *shahada*.

k. Claim spiritual freedom from the *shahada* by reciting a prayer of renunciation.

Case study: What would you do?

You have been invited to Jos, Nigeria to attend a "Faith and Justice" conference. You have your full funding and you are going as a volunteer helper for the media department. You find the discussions passionate and interesting and you are encouraged by the leadership to also sit in on and listen to small group workshop sessions. You willingly do so.

By the second day, the issue being debated in your small group is "Should Christians turn the third[10] cheek?" Two voices in your group strongly promote constant non-violence, continual pacifism, and flight from any violent context. Many more voices in your group protest this, saying, "Fearful flight and non-violence will only encourage Muslims to spread religious cleansing throughout Nigeria." Muslims, they argue, will only respect defiant resistance, firm measures of protection, and a vigilant church community. True Christians defend their homes and villages and do not flee.

Both sides use scripture to validate their convictions. They finally turn to you and say, "What do you say? Jesus said, 'Turn the other cheek.' Should we turn even the third cheek?"

What will you say?

———

In these sections we consider how Jesus responded to experiences of rejection. The life of Jesus, no less than the life of Muhammad, is a story of rejection, which comes to its climax in the cross. Muhammad responded to persecution with retribution: Christ's response was entirely different and this provides the key to freedom from Islam.

A hard beginning

Like Muhammad, Jesus' family circumstances were far from ideal. At birth the shame of illegitimacy hung over him (Matthew 1:18-25). He was born in humble circumstances, in a stable (Luke 2:7). After his

---

[10] In other words, should Christians keep turning the other check, not just once, but two or more times?

birth, King Herod attempted to kill him. Then he became a refugee, fleeing to Egypt (Matthew 2:13-18).

Jesus is questioned

When Jesus began his teaching ministry, around the age of thirty, he experienced a great deal of opposition. As with Muhammad, Jewish religious leaders asked questions of Jesus intended to challenge and undermine his authority:

> ... the Pharisees and the teachers of the law began to oppose him fiercely and to besiege him with questions, waiting to catch him in something he might say. (Luke 11:53-54)

These questions concerned:

- why Jesus was helping people on the Sabbath: this question was to show that he was breaking the law (Mark 3:2; Matthew 12:10)

- what authority he had to do the things he did (Mark 11:28; Matthew 21:23; Luke 20:2)

- whether it is lawful for a man to divorce his wife (Mark 10:2; Matthew 19:3)

- whether it is lawful to pay taxes to Caesar (Mark 12:15; Matthew 22:17; Luke 20:22)

- which is the greatest commandment (Matthew 22:36)

- whose son is the Messiah (Matthew 22:42)

- Jesus' paternity (John 8:19)

- the resurrection (Matthew 22:23-28; Luke 20:27-33)

- requests to perform signs (Mark 8:11; Matthew 12:38; 16:1).

In addition to the questions, Jesus was accused of:

- being demonized, 'having Satan', and doing miracles by Satan's power (Mark 3:22; Matthew 12:24; John 8:52; 10:20)

- having disciples who did not observe the Sabbath (Matthew 12:2) or the cleanliness rituals (Mark 7:2; Matthew 15:1-2; Luke 11:38)

- giving invalid testimony (John 8:13).

The rejectors

When we consider Jesus' life and teaching, we find that he experienced rejection from many different individuals and groups:

- King Herod tried to have him killed when he was still an infant (Matthew 2:16).

- People of his own home village at Nazareth took offense at him (Mark 6:3; Matthew 13:53-58) and tried to throw him off a cliff to kill him (Luke 4:28-30).

- His own family members accused him of being out of his mind (Mark 3:21).

- Many of his followers deserted him (John 6:66).

- A crowd tried to stone him (John 10:31).

- Religious leaders plotted to kill him (John 11:50).

- He was betrayed by Judas, one of his inner circle (Mark 14:43-45; Matthew 26:14-16; Luke 22:1-6; John 18:2-3).

- He was disowned three times by Peter, his chief disciple (Mark 14:66-72; Matthew 26:69-75; Luke 22:54-62; John 18).

- His crucifixion was demanded by a crowd in Jerusalem, a city which only a few days earlier had welcomed him with shouts of joy as a potential Messiah (Mark 15:12-15; Luke 23:18-23; John 19:15).

- He was punched, spat upon, and mocked by religious leaders (Mark 14:65; Matthew 26:67-68).

- He was mocked and abused by guards and Roman soldiers (Mark 15:16-20; Matthew 27:27-31; Luke 22:63-65, 23:11).

- He was falsely charged before Jewish and Roman tribunals, and sentenced to death (Mark 14:53-65; Matthew 26:57-67; John 18:28ff).

- He was crucified, the most degrading means of execution available to the Romans, which was regarded by Jews as a punishment that incurred God's curse (Deuteronomy 21:23).

- Crucified between two thieves, Jesus was reviled while enduring his dying agonies on the cross (Mark 15:21-32; Matthew 27:32-44; Luke 23:32-36; John 19:23-30).

Jesus' responses to rejection

When we consider all these rejections, we do not find that Jesus is aggressive or violent in response. He does not seek revenge.

Sometimes Jesus would simply not respond to accusations against him, most famously when he was charged before his crucifixion (Matthew 27:14). The early church regarded this as the fulfillment of a Messianic prophecy:

> He was oppressed and afflicted, yet he did not open his mouth; he was led like a lamb to the slaughter, and as a sheep before her shearers is silent, so he did not open his mouth. (Isaiah 53:7)

When he was challenged to prove himself, Jesus would sometimes refuse to do so, preferring to ask a question instead (for example, Matthew 21:24; 22:15-20).

Jesus was not quarrelsome, though many times people tried to pick fights with him:

> He will not quarrel or cry out; no one will hear his voice in the streets. A bruised reed he will not break, and a smoldering wick he will not snuff out, till he leads justice to victory. (Matthew 12:19-20, quoting Isaiah 42:1-4)

When people wanted to stone Jesus or kill him, he would just move on to another place (Luke 4:30), except for the events leading to his crucifixion, when Jesus went deliberately to his death.

The point about these responses is that when Jesus was tempted by experiences of rejection, he overcame the temptation, and did not succumb to the rejection. The letter to the Hebrews summarizes his responses as follows:

> … we do not have a high priest who is unable to empathize with our weaknesses, but we have one who has been tempted in every way, just as we are—yet he did not sin. (Hebrews 4:15)

The picture we have of Jesus in the Gospels is of someone who was very secure and at ease with himself. He was not vengeful: he felt no need to attack or destroy those who come against him. Jesus not only reacted well to rejection; he also taught his disciples a theological framework for responding to rejection, indeed for rejecting rejection. Key elements of this theology are described later in this lesson.

Two tales of rejection

It is remarkable that Jesus and Muhammad, the founders of the two largest religions of the world, are both reported to have sustained severe experiences of rejection. These commenced with the circumstances of their birth and infancy, and extended to include dealings with family members and religious authorities. Both were accused of being insane and controlled by evil forces. Both were mocked and reviled. Both suffered betrayal. Both suffered threats to their lives.

However, these remarkable similarities are overshadowed by an even more remarkable difference, which had a profound impact on the way in which these two religions were established. Whereas Muhammad's life story demonstrates the full range of negative rejection responses common to humanity, including self-rejection, self-validation, and aggression, the life of Jesus went in a completely different direction. He overcame rejection, not by imposing it upon others, but by embracing it, and thereby, according to Christian belief, overcoming its power and healing its pain. If the life of Muhammad contains the keys to understanding the imprisoning spiritual legacy of the *sharia*, how much more the life of Christ offers keys to freedom and wholeness, both for people leaving Islam and for Christians who are living in *sharia* conditions.

In these next sections we examine how Jesus understood rejection in light of his mission as Messiah and Savior, and how his life and his cross can free us from the bitter consequences of rejection.

Embrace rejection

Jesus made clear that it was an essential part of his vocation as God's Messiah to be rejected. God planned to use the rejected one as the keystone for the whole of his building:

The stone the builders rejected has become the capstone …
(Mark 12:10, citing Psalm 118:22-23; see also Matthew 21:42)

Jesus was identified (for example, 1 Peter 2:21ff and Acts 8:32-35) as the rejected, suffering servant of Isaiah, through whose sufferings people would find peace and salvation from their sins:

He was despised and rejected by men,
a man of sorrows, and familiar with pain.
…
But he was pierced for our transgressions,
he was crushed for our iniquities;
the punishment that brought us peace was upon him,
and by his wounds we are healed. (Isaiah 53:3-5)

The cross was the central part of this plan, and Jesus repeatedly referred to the fact that he would be put to death:

He then began to teach them that the Son of Man must suffer many things and be rejected by the elders, chief priests and the teachers of the law, and that he must be killed and after three days rise again. He spoke plainly about this … (Mark 8:31-32; see also Mark 10:32-34; Matthew 16:21; 20:17-19; 26:2; Luke 18:31; John 12:23)

Reject violence

Jesus explicitly and repeatedly condemned the use of force to achieve his goals, even when his own life was at stake:

"Put your sword back into its place," Jesus said to him, "for all who draw the sword will die by the sword." (Matthew 26:52)

As Jesus goes to the cross, he renounces the use of force to vindicate his mission, even at the cost of his death:

Jesus said, "My kingdom is not of this world. If it were, my servants would have fought to prevent my arrest by the Jews. But now my kingdom is from another place." (John 18:36)

When Jesus was speaking about the future sufferings of the church he did refer to bringing "a sword" when he said:

Do not suppose that I have come to bring peace to the earth. I did not come to bring peace, but a sword. (Matthew 10:34)

This is sometimes given as evidence that Jesus licensed violence; however, it in fact refers to the divisions that can come within families when Christians are rejected for faith in Christ: the corresponding passage in Luke has the word "division" instead of "sword" (Luke 12:51). The sword here is symbolic, standing for that which divides, separating one family member from another. Another possible interpretation, in the broader context of the advice Jesus was giving about future persecutions, is that the "sword" refers to persecution of Christians. In this case, this is a sword raised against Christians because of their testimony, not by them against others.

Jesus' rejection of violence was contrary to commonly held expectations about what the Messiah would do when he came to save God's people. The hope had been that this salvation would be military and political as well as spiritual. Jesus rejected the military option. He also made clear that his kingdom was not political either, when he said it was "not of this world." He taught that people should give Caesar what is Caesar's, and God what is God's (Matthew 22:21). He denied that the Kingdom of God could be located physically, because it was to be found within people (Luke 17:21).

When confronted by his disciples, who were arguing about who would get the preferred political office in the Kingdom of God— symbolized by the location of their seating position—Jesus told them that God's kingdom was not like the political kingdoms they were familiar with, where people lorded it over each other. In order to be first, he said, you had to be last (Matthew 20:16, 27), and his followers should seek to serve rather than to be served (Mark 10:43; Matthew 20:26-27).

The early church took Jesus' teachings on violence to heart. For example, early believers in the first centuries of the church were prohibited from engaging in some professions, including that of a soldier, and if a Christian did happen to be a soldier, he was prohibited from killing.

Love your enemies

One of the damaging reactions to rejection can be aggression. This is driven by the enmity which the experience of rejection can cause. Jesus, however, taught that:

- retribution is no longer acceptable—evil actions should be met with good in return, not evil (Matthew 5:38-42)

- it is wrong to judge others (Matthew 7:1-5)

- enemies are to be loved, not hated (Matthew 5:44)

- the meek will inherit the earth (Matthew 5:5)

- peacemakers will be called children of God (Matthew 5:9).

These teachings were not mere words that the disciples listened to and then forgot. Jesus' followers made it clear in their letters, which are preserved in the New Testament, that these principles guided them even in the face of great trials and opposition:

> To this very hour we go hungry and thirsty, we are in rags, we are brutally treated, we are homeless ... When we are cursed, we bless; when we are persecuted, we endure it; when we are slandered, we answer kindly. (1 Corinthians 4:11-13; see also 1 Peter 3:10; Titus 3:1-2; Romans 12:14-21)

The apostles showed believers the example of Jesus himself (1 Peter 2:21-25). This was so influential that in the writings of the early church the "love your enemies" verse of Matthew 5:44 became the most frequently quoted passage of the Bible.

Prepare yourselves for persecution

Jesus taught his followers that persecution was inevitable: they would be flogged, hated, betrayed, and put to death (Mark 13:9-13; Luke 21:12-19; Matthew 10:17-23).

He warned his disciples, when training them how to take his message to others, that they would experience rejection. In sharp contrast to the example and teaching of Muhammad, which encouraged Muslims to respond to suffering with violence and even slaughter, Jesus taught his disciples to simply "shake the dust off your feet when you leave." In other words, they should just move on, taking nothing evil or impure away from their encounter (Mark 6:11; Matthew 10:14). This was not a parting in bitterness, so their peace would "return" to them (Matthew 10:13-14).

Jesus himself modeled this when a Samaritan village refused to welcome him. His disciples asked him whether he wanted them to call down fire from heaven upon the Samaritans, but Jesus rebuked his disciples and just moved on (Luke 9:54-56).

Jesus taught his disciples that they were to flee to another place when persecuted (Matthew 10:23). They should not worry, because the Holy Spirit would help them to know what to say (Matthew 10:19-20; Luke 12:11-12, 21:14-15), and neither should they be afraid (Matthew 10:26, 31).

A distinctive teaching of Jesus was that his followers should rejoice when they are persecuted, because they will be identifying with the prophets:

> Blessed are you when people hate you, when they exclude you and insult you and reject your name as evil, because of the Son of Man. Rejoice in that day and leap for joy, because great is your reward in heaven. For that is how their ancestors treated the prophets. (Luke 6:22-23; see also Matthew 5:11-12)

There is plenty of evidence that this message was wholeheartedly embraced by the early church, as part of their devotion to Christ:

> … even if you should suffer for what is right, you are blessed. (1 Peter 3:14; also 2 Corinthians 1:5; Philippians 2:17-18; 1 Peter 4:12-14)

Jesus also encouraged his disciples with the hope that, along with persecution, they would receive the gift of eternal life, but to receive this promise in the next life they had to remain faithful in this life (Mark 10:29-30, 13:13).

Reconciliation

In Christian understanding, the essential human problem is sin, which alienates humanity from God and from each other. The problem of sin is not just an issue of disobedience. It is a breach in relationship with God. When Adam and Eve disobeyed God they turned away from him. They chose not to trust God but to listen to the serpent. They turned their backs on God, rejecting him, and rejecting relationship with him. As a result, God rejected them and excluded them from his presence. They became subject to the curses of the Fall.

In the history of Israel, God provided a covenant through Moses to re-establish right relationship between God and humankind, but his people disobeyed the commandments and went their own way. In their disobedience, they rejected relationship with God and came under judgment. But God did not reject them utterly: he had a plan for their restoration. He had a plan for their salvation and for the salvation of the world.

Although people rejected God, he did not finally reject them. His heart yearned for the people he had made, and he had a plan for their reconciliation. The incarnation and cross of Jesus Christ are the fulfillment of this plan for the restoration of all humanity in healed relationship with God.

The cross is the key to overcoming the deep issue of human rejection of God and the judgment this brings. Jesus' submission to rejection, through the cross, provides the key to overcoming rejection itself. The power of rejection is in the reactions that it tends to trigger in the hearts of people everywhere. By absorbing the hatred of his attackers, and giving his life as a sacrifice for the sins of the world, Jesus defeated the power of rejection itself, overwhelming it with love. This love that Jesus showed was none other than the love of God for the world that he had made:

> For God so loved the world that he gave his one and only Son, that whoever believes in him shall not perish but have eternal life. (John 3:16)

In his death on the cross, Jesus took upon himself the punishment that humanity deserved for rejecting God. This penalty was death, and Christ bore it so that all people who believe in him will find forgiveness and eternal life. In this way Jesus also overcame the power of rejection, by satisfying its penalty.

In the Torah it was the shedding of blood of sacrificial animals that atoned for sin. This symbolism is applied by Christians to understand the meaning of Jesus' death on the cross. This is expressed in Isaiah's song of the suffering servant:

... the punishment that bought us peace was upon him, and by his wounds we are healed ... Yet it was the Lord's will to crush him and cause him to suffer, and though the Lord makes his life an offering for sin, he will see his offspring and prolong his days ... he poured out his life unto death, and was numbered with the transgressors. For he bore the sin of many, and made intercession for the transgressors. (Isaiah 53:5, 10, 12)

In a powerful passage from his letter to the Romans, Paul explained how the sacrifice of Christ brings an end to rejection by granting us its opposite, reconciliation:

For if, when we were God's enemies, we were reconciled to him through the death of his Son, how much more, having been reconciled, shall we be saved through his life! Not only is this so, but we also rejoice in God through our Lord Jesus Christ, through whom we have now received reconciliation. (Romans 5:10-11)

This reconciliation also overcomes all rights of condemnation which might be raised by third parties, including human beings, angels, or demons (Romans 8:38):

Who will bring any charge against those whom God has chosen? It is God who justifies ... [Nothing] will be able to separate us from the love of God that is in Christ Jesus our Lord. (Romans 8:33, 39)

Not only this, but Christians have been entrusted with the ministry of reconciliation, both through extending reconciliation to others and also through proclaiming the message of the cross and its power to destroy rejection:

All this is from God, who reconciled us to himself through Christ and gave us the ministry of reconciliation; that God was reconciling the world to himself in Christ, not counting people's sins against them. And he has committed to us the message of reconciliation. We are therefore Christ's ambassadors, as though God were making his appeal through us. (2 Corinthians 5:18-20)

Resurrection

One of the persistent themes of Muhammad's 'revelations' and his many statements was a desire for vindication or self-validation. He achieved this for himself by forcing his enemies to submit to his creed, so that they placed themselves under his guidance and authority, or else by compelling them to accept dhimmitude. Their third alternative was death.

In the Christian understanding of the mission of Christ, there is vindication, but it is not achieved by Christ for himself. The role of the suffering Messiah was to humble himself, embracing rejection. Vindication came through the resurrection and ascension of Christ, through which death and all its power were defeated:

> ... he was not abandoned to the grave, nor did his body see decay. God has raised this Jesus to life, and we are all witnesses of the fact. Exalted to the right hand of God, he has received from the Father the promised Holy Spirit and has poured out what you now see and hear ... God has made this Jesus ... both Lord and Christ. (Acts 2:31-36)

A famous passage from Paul's letter to the Philippians describes how Jesus "humbled himself," willingly adopting a slave's role. His obedience extended even to death. But God exalted him to a spiritual position of supreme authority. This victory was not due to Christ's own striving but to God's vindication of Christ's supreme sacrifice upon the cross:

> ... have the same mindset as Christ Jesus: who, being in very nature God, did not consider equality with God something to be used to his own advantage; rather, he made himself nothing by taking the very nature of a servant, being made in human likeness.
>
> And being found in appearance as a man, he humbled himself by becoming obedient to death—even death on a cross!
>
> Therefore God exalted him to the highest place and gave him the name that is above every name, that at the name of Jesus every knee should bow ... (Philippians 2:4-10)

The discipleship of the cross

For Christians, to follow Christ means identifying with his death and resurrection. Both Jesus and his followers repeatedly refer to the need to "die" with Christ—that is, to put the old way of living to death—and be reborn, raised to a new life according to Christ's way of love and reconciliation, not living for ourselves, but for God. Christians regard experiences of suffering as a way of sharing in the sufferings of Christ. This defines the meaning of the trials they go through as a pathway through to eternal life, and a sign not of defeat, but of future victory. It is God who will vindicate the faithful believers, not the brutal powers of this world:

> Whoever wants to be my disciple must deny themselves and take up their cross and follow me. For whoever wants to save their life will lose it, but whoever loses their life for me and for the gospel will save it. (Mark 8:34-35; see also 1 John 3:14, 16; 2 Corinthians 5:14-15; Hebrews 12:1-2)

Muhammad against the cross

In the light of all we have learned, and knowing that we live in a spiritual world, we should not be surprised to learn that Muhammad hated crosses. A *hadith* reported that if ever Muhammad found an object in his house with the mark of a cross on it, he would destroy it.[11]

As we saw in Lesson 3, Muhammad's hatred of the cross even extended to teaching that Isa, the Islamic Jesus, will return to the earth as a cross-destroying prophet of Islam, to eliminate Christianity from the face of the earth.

Today Muhammad's enmity to the cross is shared by many Muslims. In many parts of the world today Christian crosses are hated, banned, and destroyed by Muslims.

This even meant that Archbishop of Canterbury George Carey was compelled to agree to remove his cross from around his neck when his plane had to make a forced stop in Saudi Arabia in 1995. The

---

11. W. Muir, *The Life of Muhammad*, vol. 3, p. 61, note 47.

incident was described by David Skidmore in the Episcopal News Service:

> Carey's flight out of Cairo for Sudan was forced to make an intermediary stop in Saudi Arabia. On the approach to the Red Sea coastal city of Jidda, Saudi Arabia, Carey was told to remove all religious insignia, including his clerical collar and pectoral cross.

Yet although the cross is rejected by Muslims, for Christians it stands for our freedom.

In these sections we consider a prayer of commitment to follow Jesus Christ, some testimonies of freedom, and a prayer for being set free from the power of Islam and the *shahada* covenant. These prayers are specifically intended for people who are choosing to leave Islam to follow Jesus of Nazareth, as well as for people who have already chosen to follow Jesus and desire to claim their freedom from all the principles and powers of Islam.

Follow Jesus

You are invited to affirm your commitment to follow Christ by reading this prayer out loud. Review this carefully before you read it, so you can be sure of what you are saying.

As you consider this prayer, please note that it includes the following elements:

1. *Two confessions:*

    ▪ I am a sinner and cannot save myself.

    ▪ There is only one God, the creator, who sent his Son Jesus to die for my sins.

2. *Turning away* (repenting) from my sins and from all that is evil.

3. *Requests* for forgiveness, freedom, eternal life, and the Holy Spirit.

4. *Transfer of allegiance* to Christ as Lord of my life.

5. *Promise and consecration* of my life to submit to and serve Christ.

6. *Declaration* of my identity in Christ.

Declaration and Prayer of Commitment to Follow Jesus Christ

I believe in one God, the creator, almighty Father.

I renounce all other so-called 'gods'.

I acknowledge that I have sinned against God and against other people. In this I have disobeyed God and rebelled against him and his laws.

I cannot rescue myself from my sins.

I believe Jesus is the Christ, the risen Son of God. He died on the cross in my place and took upon himself the judgment for my sins. He was raised from the dead for me.

I turn away from my sins.

I ask for Christ's gift of forgiveness, won on the cross.

I receive this gift of forgiveness now.

I choose to accept God as my Father, and desire to become his.

I seek the gift of eternal life.

I hand over the rights to my life to Christ and invite him to rule as Lord of my life from this day on.

I renounce all other spiritual allegiances. I specifically renounce the shahada and all its claims over me.

I reject Satan and all evil. I break all ungodly agreements I have made with evil spirits or principles of evil.

I renounce all ungodly ties to others who have exercised an ungodly authority over me.

I renounce all ungodly covenants made by my ancestors on my behalf, which have impacted upon me in any way.

I renounce all psychic or spiritual abilities that do not come from God through Jesus Christ.

I ask for the gift of the promised Holy Spirit.

Father God, please free and transform me so I can bring glory to you and you alone.

Release in me the fruit of the Holy Spirit so I can honor you and love others.

I declare before human witnesses and before all spiritual authorities that I consecrate and bind myself to God through Jesus Christ.

I declare that I am a citizen of heaven. God is my protector. With the help of the Holy Spirit I choose to submit to and follow Jesus Christ and him alone as Lord all my days.

Amen.

Testimonies of freedom

Here are some testimonies of people who were set free using the prayers in this lesson.

A discipleship course

A ministry in North America was running regular intensive training for people of a Muslim background who had accepted Christ as their Lord and Savior. The course coordinators found that the participants were experiencing many persistent discipleship difficulties. They became aware of the prayers in this book for renouncing the *shahada* and decided to invite all course participants to use these prayers to renounce Islam together. The participants' response was one of great relief and joy. They asked, "Why didn't anyone explain that we needed to renounce Islam? We should have done this long ago!" After that, the renunciation of Islam became an essential part of their training course.

Middle East Christians who renounced the shahada

Here are two testimonies of Muslim converts in the Middle East after they had renounced the *shahada*:

I feel truly free, as if the yoke that was tied around my neck is loosened and broken. This prayer is more than wonderful. I feel like a caged animal that has been set free. I feel the freedom.

I was deeply in need of this and it was as if you knew what was going on in my mind ... as I said the prayer again and again I felt a strange comfort that goes beyond words; as if a heavy burden has been removed and I'm totally freed. What a liberating feeling!

Truth encounter

The first step in preparing yourself to renounce the *shahada* (or the *dhimma*) is to consider certain verses of scripture. We do this to affirm an important truth, which underpins our prayers. This can be called a 'truth encounter'.

What scriptural truth do these verses from 1 John and John's Gospel teach us to trust and pray for?

> And so we know and rely on the love God has for us. God is love. Whoever lives in love lives in God, and God in him. (1 John 4:16)

> [Jesus said:] For God so loved the world that he gave his one and only Son, that whoever believes in him shall not perish but have eternal life. (John 3:16)

They teach us that God's love overcomes rejection.

What divine truth do these two verses teach us to embrace and pray for?

> For God did not give us a spirit of fear, but a spirit of power, of love and of self-control. (2 Timothy 1:7)

> The Spirit you received does not make you slaves, so that you live in fear again; rather, the Spirit you received brought about your adoption to sonship. And by him we cry, "Abba, Father." The Spirit himself testifies with our spirit that we are God's children. Now if we are children, then we are heirs—heirs of God and co-heirs with Christ, if indeed we share in his sufferings in order that we may also share in his glory. (Romans 8:15-17)

They teach us that our inheritance is not intimidation: it is in God.

What truth do these two verses teach us to believe and pray for?

> [Jesus said:] Then you will know the truth, and the truth will set you free. (John 8:32)

> It is for freedom Christ has set us free. Stand firm, then, and do not let yourselves be burdened again by a yoke of slavery. (Galatians 5:1)

They teach us that we are called to live in freedom.

What truth do these two verses teach us to trust and pray for?

> Do you not know that your bodies are temples of the Holy Spirit, who is in you, whom you have received from God? You are not your own; you were bought at a price. Therefore honor God with your bodies. (1 Corinthians 6:19-20)

> They triumphed over him by the blood of the Lamb ... (Revelation 12:11)

They teach us that our bodies belong to God and not to oppression: our blood price has already been paid.

What biblical truth does this verse teach us to claim and pray for?

> ... there is neither Jew nor Greek, neither slave nor free, nor is there male and female, for you are all one in Christ Jesus. (Galatians 3:28)

It teaches us that men and women are equal before God, and one group is not superior to another.

What divine truth do these three passages teach us to believe and pray for?

> But thanks be to God, who always leads us as captives in Christ's triumphal procession and uses us to spread the aroma of the knowledge of him everywhere. For we are to God the pleasing aroma of Christ among those who are being saved and those who are perishing. (2 Corinthians 2:14-15)

> I have given them the glory that you gave me, that they may be one as we are one—I in them and you in me—so that they may be brought to complete unity. Then the world will know that

you sent me and have loved them even as you have loved me. (John 17:22-23)

[Jesus said:] Whoever wants to be my disciple must deny themselves and take up their cross daily and follow me. (Luke 9:23)

They teach us that our distinctive features are not humiliation or inferiority, but Christ's victory, unity in Christ's love, and the cross.

What scriptural truth do these verses teach us to embrace and pray for?

[Jesus said:] Unless I go away, the Advocate will not come to you; but if I go, I will send him to you. When he comes, he will prove the world to be in the wrong about sin and righteousness and judgment ... (John 16:7-8)

[Jesus said:] But when he, the Spirit of truth, comes, he will guide you into all the truth. (John 16:13)

They teach us that we have the power of the Holy Spirit to reveal the truth.

What truth does this verse teach us to believe and pray for?

... fixing our eyes on Jesus, the pioneer and perfecter of faith. For the joy set before him he endured the cross, scorning its shame, and sat down at the right hand of the throne of God. (Hebrews 12:2)

It teaches us that we have authority to follow Christ in overcoming shame.

What divine truth does this verse teach us to trust and pray for?

Only be careful, and watch yourselves closely so that you do not forget the things your eyes have seen or let them fade from your heart as long as you live. Teach them to your children and to their children after them. (Deuteronomy 4:9)

It teaches us that we have the right and the responsibility to educate ourselves and our children about spiritual matters.

What scriptural truth do these verses teach us to embrace and pray for?

The tongue has the power of life and death, and those who love it will eat its fruit. (Proverbs 18:21)

Now, Lord, consider their threats and enable your servants to speak your word with great boldness. (Acts 4:29)

Love does not delight in evil but rejoices with the truth. (1 Corinthians 13:6)

If anyone acknowledges that Jesus is the Son of God, God lives in them and they in God. (1 John 4:15)

So do not throw away your confidence; it will be richly rewarded. (Hebrews 10:35)

They teach us that we have authority in Christ to speak the truth in love, with boldness.

What biblical truth do these verses teach us to believe and pray for?

... God's testimony is greater because it is the testimony of God, which he has given about his Son. (1 John 5:9)

They triumphed ... by the word of their testimony. (Revelation 12:11)

They teach us that we can have complete confidence in the word of truth.

What divine truth do these verses teach us to claim and pray for?

Finally be strong in the Lord and in his mighty power. Put on the full armor of God, so that you can take your stand against the devil's schemes. (Ephesians 6:10-11)

For though we live in the world, we do not wage war as the world does. The weapons we fight with are not the weapons of the world. On the contrary, they have divine power to demolish strongholds. We demolish arguments and every pretension that sets itself up against the knowledge of God, and we take captive every thought to make it obedient to Christ. (2 Corinthians 10:3-5)

They teach us that we are not defenseless or weaponless, but are spiritually armed in Christ.

What does this verse teach us to trust and pray for?

Consider it pure joy, my brothers and sisters, whenever you face trials of many kinds ... (James 1:2; see also Philippians 1:29)

It teaches us that we should consider it a joy to suffer in Christ's name.

What scriptural truth do these verses teach us to embrace and pray for?

[Jesus said:] ... now the prince of this world will be driven out, but I, when I am lifted up from the earth, will draw all people to myself. (John 12:31-32)

They teach us that the cross destroys Satan's power and draws us to freedom in Christ.

What biblical truth do these verses teach us to claim and pray for?

When you were dead in your sins and in the uncircumcision of your flesh, God made you alive with Christ. He forgave us all our sins, having canceled the charge of our legal indebtedness, which stood against us and condemned us; he has taken it away, nailing it to the cross. And having disarmed the powers and authorities, he made a public spectacle of them, triumphing over them by the cross. (Colossians 2:13-15)

They teach us that the cross cancels ungodly covenants and destroys all their power.

Before praying, we need to understand that our prayers and declarations are powerful and effective. Choose to agree with God that it is his will to bring you into complete freedom. Agree in your spirit to accept the truth that Christ has accepted you, and wants to set you free from all the snares of the evil one. Resolve to confront and reject the lies of Islam's covenants.

This is a prayer to renounce the *shahada*. It is best read standing.

Declaration and Prayer to Renounce the *Shahada* and Break Its Power

I renounce the false submission as taught and demonstrated by Muhammad.

I renounce and reject as false the belief that Muhammad is a messenger from God.

I reject the claim that the Quran is God's Word.

I reject and renounce the shahada and every recitation of it.

I renounce saying al-Fatihah. I renounce its claims that Jews are under the wrath of God, and Christians have gone astray.

I renounce hatred of the Jews. I reject the claim that they have corrupted the Bible.

I reject the claim that God has rejected the Jews, and declare it to be a lie.

I renounce reciting the Quran and reject its authority over my life.

I renounce all false worship based on Muhammad's example.

I renounce all the false teachings about God which Muhammad brought, and the claim that Allah as portrayed in the Quran is God.

[For people from a Shi'a background: *I reject and renounce all ties to Ali and the twelve caliphs. I renounce all grief on behalf of Hussein and Islamic martyrs.*]

I renounce my dedication to Islam when I was born, and the dedication of my ancestors.

I specifically reject and renounce Muhammad's example. I renounce violence, intimidation, hatred, a spirit of offense, deception, superiority, rape, abuse of women, theft, and all the sins that Muhammad committed.

I reject and renounce shame. I declare that there is no condemnation in Christ Jesus and the blood of Christ cleanses me from all shame.

I reject and renounce all fear incited by Islam. I ask God's forgiveness for having entertained fears due to Islam, and choose to trust in the God and Father of my Lord Jesus Christ in all things.

I reject and renounce cursing of others. I choose to be a person of blessing.

I reject and renounce all ties with the jinn. I reject Islamic teaching about the qarin, and cut all ties with demons.

I choose to walk by the Spirit, with God's Word as a light for my path.

I seek God's forgiveness for any and all ungodly deeds I committed because of following Muhammad as a messenger of Allah.

I reject and renounce the blasphemous claim that when Jesus returns he will compel all people on the earth to follow the sharia of Muhammad.

I choose to follow Christ and him alone.

I confess that Christ is the Son of God, that he died on the cross for my sins, and was raised from the dead for my salvation. I praise God for the cross of Christ, and choose to take up my cross and follow him.

I confess that Christ is Lord of all. He rules over the heavens and the earth. He is Lord of my life. I confess that he will come again to judge the living and the dead. I cling to Christ and declare that there is no other name in heaven or on earth by which I must be saved.

I invite my Father God to give me a new heart, the heart of Christ, to guide me and bless me in all I do and say.

I reject all false worship, and dedicate my body to the worship of the living God, the Father, Son, and Holy Spirit.

Amen.

Study Guide

Lesson 5

Since the teaching in this lesson is focused on Jesus and the Bible, there are no quranic references, no new vocabulary, and no new names.

The Bible verses are included in the questions that follow.

Questions Lesson 5

- Discuss the case study.

A hard beginning

1. What do the lives of Jesus and Muhammad have in common?

2. In what four ways was the beginning of Jesus' life painful?

   1)

   2)

   3)

   4)

Jesus is questioned

3. With what questions did the Pharisees attack Christ?

- Mark 3:2, etc. questions about …
- Mark 11:28, etc. questions about …
- Mark 10:2, etc. questions about …
- Mark 12:15, etc. questions about …
- Matthew 22:36, questions about …
- Matthew 22:42, questions about …
- John 8:19, questions about …
- Matthew 22:23-28, etc. questions about …
- Mark 8:11, etc. questions about …
- Mark 3:22, etc. questions about …
- Matthew 12:2, etc. questions about …
- John 8:13, questions about …

The rejectors

4. What forms of rejection did Jesus experience?

   - Matthew 2:16 …
   - Mark 6:3, etc. …
   - Mark 3:21 …
   - John 6:66 …
   - John 10:31 …
   - John 11:50 …
   - Mark 14:43-45, etc. …

- Mark 14:66-72, etc. …
- Mark 15:12-15, etc. …
- Mark 14:65, etc. …
- Mark 15:16-20, etc. …
- Mark 14:53-65, etc. …
- Deuteronomy 21:23 …
- Mark 15:21-32, etc. …

Jesus' responses to rejection

5. What six things does Durie note that are astonishing about how Jesus responded to rejection? (Based on Matthew 27:14; Isaiah 53:7; Matthew 21:24; Matthew 22:15-20; Matthew 12:19-20; Isaiah 42:1-4; Luke 4:30.)

1)

2)

3)

4)

5)

6)

6. How did Jesus uniquely respond when tempted by rejection? (Based on Hebrews 4:15.)

7. Why did Jesus not feel the need to attack or destroy those who came against him?

Embrace rejection

8. By God's planning, what was an essential part of Jesus' vocation as God's Messiah? (Based on Mark 12:10, etc. and Isaiah 52:3-5.)

9. What was a central part of God's plan? (Based on Mark 8:31-32, etc.)

Reject violence

10. What does Jesus reject, according to Matthew 26:52 and John 18:36?

11. How does Durie understand the "bringing of a sword" from Matthew 10:34?

12. What views, to the disappointment of some of his followers, did Jesus reject about the Messiah? (Based on Matthew 22:21; Luke 17:21; Matthew 20:16; Mark 10:43; Matthew 20:26-27.)

13. How did the early church apply this teaching to soldiers who became Christians?

Love your enemies

14. What did Jesus teach about how to treat others?

1) Matthew 5:38-42, concerning retribution for evil ...

2) Matthew 7:1-5, concerning judging ...

3) Matthew 5:44, concerning enemies ...

4) Matthew 5:5, concerning meekness ...

5) Matthew 5:9, concerning peacemakers ...

6) 1 Corinthians 4:11ff, etc. concerning persecution ...

7) 1 Peter 2:21-25, concerning our example ...

Prepare yourselves for persecution

15. What did Jesus teach his followers about what would be inevitable? (Based on Mark 13:9-13, etc.)

16. While Muhammad taught his followers to repay suffering with violence, how did Jesus instruct his followers? (Based on Mark 6:11; Matthew 10:13-14.)

17. When did Jesus model the need to move on without being bitter? (Based on Luke 9:54-56.)

18. What three things did Jesus teach his disciples to do when violently persecuted? (Based on Matthew 10:19-20, etc.)

   1)

   2)

   3)

19. What was a fourth distinctive teaching of Jesus to his disciples facing persecution? (Based on Luke 6:22-23, etc.)

20. What was the fifth truth taught to persecuted disciples? (Based on 1 Peter 3:14, etc.)

Reconciliation

21. Durie notes that Adam and Eve's sin had three results for humankind. What were they?

22. What is the fulfillment of God's plan to restore humanity and heal the God–human relationship?

23. What provides the key to overcoming rejection?

24. How did Jesus defeat the power of rejection? (Based upon John 3:16.)

25. Which Old Testament symbolism and which prophecy does Jesus' death on the cross point back to?

26. In bringing rejection to an end, what did Christ's sacrifice grant us?

27. According to Romans 8, what more does reconciliation overcome?

28. According to 2 Corinthians 5, what ministry has God entrusted to us so that we may destroy the power of rejection?

Resurrection

29. What did Muhammad desire to do to his enemies?

30. According to Acts 2:31-36, how did Christ achieve vindication?

31. According to Durie's insight from Philippians 2:4-10, what does God grant Christ for humbling himself and offering himself upon the cross?

The discipleship of the cross

32. When Christ's disciples 'take up their cross', how do they interpret their experiences of suffering? (Based upon Mark 8:34-35, etc.)

Muhammad against the cross

33. How much did Muhammad hate crosses?

34. According to Islam, what choice will allegedly disappear once Isa (the Islamic Jesus) returns to earth?

35. What humiliating demand was placed upon the English Archbishop George Carey when he flew into Saudi Arabia?

For the prayers section, please follow the following steps:

1. First all the participants recite together the 'Declaration and Prayer of Commitment to Follow Jesus Christ'.

2. Then the testimonies and 'truth encounter' verses are read to all participants.

3. After this, all participants stand together and recite the 'Declaration and Prayer to Renounce the *Shahada* and Break Its Power'.

4. For more detailed instructions, see the Guide for Leaders.

6

Freedom from the *Dhimma*

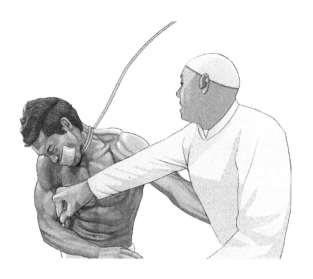

"His blood speaks a truer word."
Hebrews 12:24

Lesson objectives

a. Grasp the theological foundation of the *dhimma* covenant imposed by Muslims upon a conquered people.

b. Comprehend the three choices that Muslims required of subjugated people and the impact of the "third choice".

c. Explain the implications of the *dhimma* covenant for non-Muslims.

d. Consider examples of *dhimma* subjugation from Islamic literature and eyewitnesses.

e. Grasp the psychological and spiritual impact of the annual ritual of decapitation.

f. Consider examples of how dhimmitude is returning to the West today.

g. Understand why certain people need to renounce the *dhimma* covenant.

h. Briefly review how differently Jesus and Muhammad responded to rejection.

i. Understand why prayers for renouncing the *dhimma* covenant are needed for certain Christians.

j. Briefly list negative spiritual influences of dhimmitude.

k. Consider scriptural verses declaring 15 specific truths as you prepare to renounce the *shahada* (if not already done in the previous lesson).

l. Claim spiritual freedom from the *dhimma* by reciting a prayer of renunciation, including a prayer of confession and 35 unique declarations and renunciations.

Case study: What would you do?

You and your friends are invited to attend a prayer conference at a retreat center. You are eager to go and as you meet the other people, you are very excited to see so many Christians from a Muslim background.

At the end of the first evening session, you are instructed to join groups of 10-12 people to share needs and to pray for 30 minutes. Your group has several Muslim Background Believers. Several of them open up and share how happy they are to join other Christians. However, a few Christians in the group begin to share how much hurt, fear, shame, and even hatred they have suffered from Muslims who have abused them as inferiors and infidels, and have marginalized them in their village. The former Muslims reply, "Well, we're sorry to hear that but just forgive them; these Muslims probably didn't know what they were doing."

You can see that this reply has hurt those who have shared their pain. They turn to you and others in the group and ask, "Is it not true that it goes deeper than just saying, 'I forgive you'? We have forgiven them, but we still feel very uncomfortable, even fearful, of any Muslim." You can see that these last words are now making the former Muslims very upset.

What will you say and do?

In this lesson we consider Islam's policy toward and treatment of non-Muslims who come under Islamic rule. These people, including Christians and Jews, are known in Islam as *dhimmis.*

The *dhimma* covenant

In 2006, when Pope Benedict gave his famous Regensburg lecture, he quoted Byzantine Emperor Manuel II Palaeologus, who spoke of Muhammad's "command to spread by the sword the faith he preached."

The Pope's comments got an angry reaction from Muslims. After this speech, around 100 people were killed in riots around the world. One of the most interesting responses was from Sheikh Abdul Aziz al-Sheikh, Grand Mufti of Saudi Arabia, who issued a press release stating that Islam was not spread by violence. He argued that it was wrong to accuse Islam of this, because infidels had a third choice. The first option was Islam, the second was the sword, and the third was to "surrender and pay tax, and they will be allowed to remain in their land, observing their religion under the protection of Muslims."

The Grand Mufti referred his readers to the example of Muhammad. He said, "Those who read the Quran and *Sunna* can understand the facts."

The three choices the mufti referred to were:

1. convert to Islam;

2. the sword—kill or be killed; or

3. surrender to the forces of Islam.

The first two choices go back to Muhammad, who said:

I have been ordered (by Allah) to fight against the people until they testify that none has the right to be worshipped but Allah and that Muhammad is the messenger of Allah ... so if they perform all that, then they save their lives and property from me ...

However, this was moderated by other statements in which Muhammad gave a third option, in addition to Islam or the sword, which was to surrender, and pay tribute known as *jizya*:

Fight in the name of Allah and in the way of Allah.
Fight against those who disbelieve in Allah. Make a holy war ...
When you meet your enemies who are associators, invite them
to three courses of action.
If they respond to any one of these, you also accept it and
withhold yourself from doing them any harm.
Invite them to (accept) Islam; if they respond to you, accept it
from them and desist from fighting against them ...
If they refuse to accept Islam, demand from them the *jizya*.
If they agree to pay, accept it from them and hold off your
hands.
If they refuse to pay the tax, seek Allah's help and fight them.

The requirement to pay *jizya* is also based on a verse of the Quran:

Fight those ... who have been given the Book—until they pay
jizya [tribute] out of hand and are disgraced [made small,
belittled]. (Q9:29)

Communities that have surrendered to Islamic rule are considered by
Islamic law to have accepted a *dhimma* pact, which is a covenant of
surrender in which the non-Muslim community agrees to two things:
1) pay annual *jizya* tribute to the Muslims, and 2) be disgraced or
'made small', adopting an attitude of defeated humility.

The Muslim commentator Ibn Kathir said in his commentary on
Q9:29 that "Muslims are not allowed to honor the people of the
dhimma or elevate them above Muslims, for they are miserable,
disgraced and humiliated." This degraded condition, he stated, was to
be ensured by the laws of the *sharia*, guaranteeing "their continued
humiliation, degradation and disgrace."

In return for agreeing to the *dhimma* covenant, the *sharia* permits
non-Muslims to keep the religion that they had before conquest.
Non-Muslims who live under these conditions are known as
dhimmis.

The *dhimma* system is a political manifestation of two theological
principles in the Quran:

1. Islam should triumph over other religions:

It is he who has sent his messenger with the guidance and the religion of truth, that he may cause it to prevail over every religion. (Q48:28)

2. Muslims must be in a position of power to enforce Islam's teaching on what is right and wrong:

You are the best community brought forth for humankind, commanding right and forbidding wrong, and believing in God. (Q3:110)

Jizya

In Islamic *sharia* law the *dhimma* covenant treats non-Muslims as people whose lives would have been lost if Muslims had not spared them. This goes back to a pre-Islamic idea that if you conquered someone, and let them live, they owed you their head. Because of this, the annual *jizya* head tax, paid by adult *dhimmi* males to the Islamic state, is described in authoritative Islamic sources as a redemption paid by *dhimmis* in return for their blood. The word *jizya* means 'reparations', 'compensation' or 'tribute'. Muslim lexicographers defined its meaning as follows:

… the tax that is taken from the free non-Muslim of a Muslim government whereby they ratify the compact [the *dhimma* pact] that ensures them protection, as though it were a compensation for their not being slain.[12]

Muhammad ibn Yusuf Atfayyish, a nineteenth-century Algerian commentator, explained this principle in his commentary on Q9:29:

It was said: it [*jizya*] is a satisfaction for their blood. It is said it has sufficed … to compensate for their not being slain. Its purpose is to substitute for the duties (*wajib*) of killing and of slavery … It is for the benefit of Muslims.

Or, as William Eton explained more than a century earlier in his *Survey of the Turkish Empire*, published in 1798:

The very words of their formulary, given to the Christian subjects on their paying the capitation tax [*jizya*], import, that

---

12. Edward W. Lane, *Arabic-English Lexicon*.

the sum of money received, is taken as compensation for being permitted to wear their heads that year.

The penalty for non-compliance

In Islamic law, a severe penalty applied for non-compliance with the *dhimma* covenant. If a *dhimmi* omitted to pay the *jizya* tax, or failed to obey the regulations imposed upon *dhimmis*, the penalty was that *jihad* started again. This meant war conditions: the *dhimmis'* possessions were to be looted, the women enslaved and raped, and the men killed (or converted at the point of a sword).

A famous example of a specific *dhimma* covenant, known as the Pact of Umar, included a clause where the Christians of Syria invoked this penalty of *jihad* upon themselves:

> These are the conditions that we set against ourselves and followers of our religion in return for safety and protection. If we break any of these promises that we set for your benefit against ourselves, then our *dhimma* is broken and you are allowed to do with us what you are allowed of people of defiance and rebellion.

The same point is made by Ibn Qudama, that if a non-Muslim *dhimmi* does not comply with the conditions of the *dhimma* covenant, they forfeit their life and possessions:

> A protected person who violates his protection agreement, whether by refusing to pay the head tax [*jizya*] or to submit to the laws of the community … makes his person and his goods *halal* ['licit'—freely available to be killed or captured by Muslims].

The history of many *dhimmi* communities has been marked by traumatic historical events involving massacres, rape, and looting. These have served to keep the non-Muslims in a state of perpetual intimidation and have reinforced the psychological and spiritual bondage of the *dhimma* over the whole community. Two examples are:

- In 1066 the Jews of Granada, numbering around 3,000, were massacred by Muslims. The background was that Samuel ha-Nagid, a Jew, had been Grand Vizier of Granada, serving the

Muslim sultan. He was followed in the same office by his son, Joseph ha-Nagid. The success of these Jews was considered a breach of the *dhimma* conditions, which prohibits non-Muslims from exercising authority over Muslims. A campaign of religious incitement against the Jews, which appealed to the *dhimma* regulations, led to the massacre. The north African jurist al-Maghili later wrote that whenever Jews occupy a prominent position serving a sultan, they are in "a state of permanent rebellion against their [*dhimmi*] status, which from then on no longer protects them." In other words, their blood was halal.

- In 1860 more than 5,000 Christians of Damascus were massacred. The background was that the Ottomans had officially abolished the *dhimma* laws. This was done under political pressure from European powers. Muslim preachers in Damascus resented this improved status and declared that because Christians were no longer acting submissively as *dhimmis* their protected status was forfeited. This resulting massacre followed classical *jihad* war procedures: men were killed, women and children were enslaved, captive women were raped, and property was looted. Some escaped with their lives by converting to Islam.

A disturbing ritual

The *jizya* tax had to be paid every year by each adult male, and a particular ritual had to be followed. *Dhimmi* men were required to undergo this ritual all over the Muslim world until the twentieth century.

The ritual of the *jizya* payment included a powerful symbolism in which a Muslim would strike the *dhimmi* on the neck, and in some versions the *dhimmi* would be dragged along with a rope tied around his neck. These ritual acts signified that the *dhimmi* was paying for his life with this tax, to escape from death or slavery. The ritual was an enactment of the death by beheading from which the *jizya* payment won an annual reprieve.

Both Muslim and non-Muslim sources provide many reports of this ritual, from Morocco to Bukhara, from the ninth century to the twentieth century. The ritual continued in some Muslim countries, such as Yemen and Afghanistan, right up until the exodus of Jews to Israel in the late 1940s and early 1950s, and in recent years there have been many calls by radical Muslims for it to be brought back.

As a symbolic decapitation, the *jizya* payment ritual can be considered to be a 'blood pact' or 'blood oath' (discussed in Lesson 2), in which the participant invokes death against themselves by simulating the manner of their execution, should they ever fail to keep the conditions of their pact. Such oaths have been used for centuries in initiation ceremonies by secret societies and occult groups, and they have psycho-spiritual power to bind the people participating in these ceremonies to submission and obedience.

The *jizya* ritual symbolically demands the consent of the *dhimmi* who participates in it to forfeit his very head if he violates any of the terms of the *dhimma* covenant, which has spared his life. It is an act of self-cursing, which says in effect "You can rightfully have my head if I break any of the conditions of my covenant." Later, if a *dhimmi* violates his covenant, he has already pronounced the death penalty against himself by virtue of undergoing this public ritual, and if he is killed, it is by his own prior permission.

In these sections we consider the psychological impact of the *dhimma* system on non-Muslims.

Humble gratitude

In essence, non-Muslims are regarded in classical Islamic law as people who owe their lives to their Muslim conquerors. They are expected to adopt an attitude of gratitude and humble inferiority. Islamic commentators are quite explicit on this point.

Many *sharia* regulations were designed to impose inferiority and vulnerability upon non-Muslims. For example:

- The witness of *dhimmis* was not accepted in *sharia* courts: this made them vulnerable to all kinds of oppression.

- *Dhimmi* houses had to be lower than Muslim houses.

- *Dhimmis* were not allowed to ride horses or raise their heads above those of Muslims.

- *Dhimmis* had to get out of the way of Muslims on public roads, moving to the side of the road to let them pass.

- *Dhimmis* were allowed no means of self-defense, which made them vulnerable to acts of violence at the hands of Muslims.

- No public displays of non-Muslim religious symbols or rituals were permitted.

- No new churches could be built and damaged churches could not be repaired.

- No criticism of Islam was permitted.

- *Dhimmis* had to dress differently, wearing distinctive clothing or colored patches.

- Muslim men could marry *dhimmi* women and any children had to be raised as Muslims; however, it was forbidden for a Muslim woman to marry a *dhimmi* man.

- There were also many other laws that enforced humiliation and segregation on non-Muslim communities.

Such laws were understood as a social and legal expression of being "made small," as commanded by the Quran (Q9:29).

The *dhimma* system was designed to reduce and demean the non-Muslim communities it dominated. The eighteenth-century Moroccan commentator Ibn Ajibah described its purpose as a killing of the soul:

> [The *dhimmi*] is commanded to put his soul, good fortune and desires to death. Above all he should kill the love of life, leadership and honor. [The *dhimmi*] is to invert the longings of his soul, he is to load it down more heavily than it can bear until it is completely submissive. Thereafter nothing will be unbearable for him. He will be indifferent to subjugation or might. Poverty and wealth will be the same to him; praise and insult will be the same; preventing and yielding will be the same; lost and found will be the same. Then, when all things are the

same, it [the soul] will be submissive and yield willingly what it should give.

A psychology of inferiority

The term 'dhimmitude' is used to describe the totality of conditions that a *dhimma* covenant produces. Like sexism and racism, dhimmitude is not only expressed in legal and social structures, but in a psychology of grateful inferiority and a will to serve, which the dominated community adopts in an attempt at self-preservation.

As the great medieval Iberian Jewish scholar Maimonides put it, "We have acquiesced, both old and young, to inure ourselves to humiliation …"; and early in the twentieth century, Serbian geographer Jovan Cvijic described how the intergenerational fear of violence at the hands of the ruling Turks and Muslim Albanians psychologically altered the Christian populations of the Balkans:

> [They became] accustomed to belonging to an inferior, servile class, whose duty it is to make themselves acceptable to the master, to humble themselves before him and to please him. These people become close-mouthed, secretive, cunning; they lose all confidence in others; they grow used to hypocrisy and meanness because these are necessary in order for them to live and to avoid violent punishments.

> The direct influence of oppression and violence is manifested in almost all the Christians as feelings of fear and apprehension … In Macedonia I heard people say: "Even in our dreams we flee from the Turks and the Albanians."

Matching the inferiority of the *dhimmi* is the superiority of the Muslim, who is afforded a sense of being generous, having allowed the *dhimmi* to live and refrained from taking his possessions. As one Iranian convert to Christianity said to me, "Christianity is still viewed as the religion of an inferior class of people. Islam is the religion of masters and rulers; Christianity is the religion of slaves."

This worldview of dhimmitude is as harmful for Muslims as it is humiliating for non-Muslims. Muslims harm themselves when they establish circumstances where they have no possibility of learning to compete on an even footing. Policies of economic protectionism can cause the economy of a nation to decline; in a similar way the religious protectionism of the *dhimma* meant that Muslims came to rely upon a false sense of superiority, which ultimately weakened them, and damaged their ability to gain a true understanding of themselves and the world around them.

The system of dhimmitude produces a set of deeply ingrained attitudes on both sides from generation to generation. Just as racism can continue in nations many years after race-based slavery has been abolished, so the institution of dhimmitude continues to affect and even dominate relationships between Muslims and others, even when the *jizya* tax is but a distant memory.

The psychology of dhimmitude can even influence societies which have never fallen under *sharia* rule. This can cripple academic inquiry and damage political discourse. For example, there has been a long line-up of Western politicians who have praised Islam, declaring it to be a religion of peace, whilst at the same time expressing gratitude. Such expressions of praise and gratitude are characteristic *dhimmi* responses to Islamic rule.

Religious persecution and the *dhimma*'s return

During the nineteenth and twentieth centuries European powers forced the Muslim world to downgrade or dismantle the *dhimma* system. However, over the past century there has been a global *sharia* revival. As part of that revival, the laws and worldview of the *dhimma* have been returning all across the Muslim world, and with this has come an increasing climate of prejudice, intimidation, and discrimination against Christians and other non-Muslims. An example is Pakistan, which was founded as a nation with a secular constitution, but which later declared itself an Islamic state, reintroduced *sharia* courts, and brought in a blasphemy law which discriminates against non-Muslims. This trend to revive *sharia* has driven growing persecution of Pakistani Christians.

In the world today, wherever the *sharia* is revived, life gets worse for Christians and other non-Muslims. Today, four out of five nations where Christians are persecuted are Islamic, and the particular patterns of persecution of Christians in these places, such as restrictions on building places of worship, are supported by revival of the laws of the *dhimma* as part of the larger *sharia* revival.

In these sections we consider reasons to renounce the *dhimma* covenant and its damaging spiritual impact.

A spiritual solution

Muhammad's life was shaped by deep experiences of rejection, leading to a wounded spirit, a spirit of offense, a victim mentality, a spirit of violence, and a will to dominate others. His calls for *jihad* 'striving' were driven by this oppressed spiritual condition, which sought release through the degradation of others. The degrading *dhimma* system is the result.

In contrast, Christ was rejected, but refused to take offense, refused to take up violence, refused to dominate others, and refused to adopt a wounded spirit. His cross and resurrection defeated rejection and the powers of darkness. Christians can turn to the cross to find freedom from the legacy of the *dhimma*.

Testimonies of freedom from the *dhimma*

Here are some testimonies of people who prayed a prayer renouncing the *dhimma* covenant and found freedom.

Intergenerational fears

One woman who I prayed with suffered from fear in various areas of her life. Her ancestors had lived as *dhimmis* in Damascus, Syria a hundred years earlier, where a famous genocide of Christians took place in 1860. When I encouraged her to say prayers renouncing the *dhimma* covenant, the power of fear was broken, and she found significant relief from fear in her daily life.

Freedom from the legacy of genocide

A man from an Armenian background had ancestors who had survived the genocide by adopting Greek names and escaping through Smyrna to Egypt. The best part of a century later, this son of refugees suffered from oppressive fears on a daily basis. He could not leave home without experiencing great anxiety about whether he had locked all the doors and windows. However, when he renounced intergenerational fear associated with the trauma of past genocides, and he prayed for his release, he experienced significant spiritual healing and freedom.

Greater effectiveness in ministry to Muslims

A New Zealand woman reported to me how her ministry to Muslims was transformed after renouncing dhimmitude and the *dhimma*:

> I was powerfully set free from intimidation and fear in a personal relationship and also have moved into a much greater effectiveness of evangelism of Muslims since praying the dhimmitude prayer at your seminar. I've been reaching out to Muslims since 1989 ... Another member of the team who was also at your seminars has also found far greater effectiveness in reaching Middle Eastern women after renouncing dhimmitude.

From fear to boldness: evangelism training

A group of Arab-speaking Christians used the prayers provided in this book as part of their preparations for an outreach to Muslims who were visiting a European country as tourists. Although these Christians were in a free country, they confessed to feeling fearful about sharing their faith. The discussion of dhimmitude opened their hearts to the need for healing from fear. One leader explained, "The fear lives inside you because of the covenant made on your behalf." After discussing the explanations of the *dhimma* covenant, people prayed prayers for freedom and together renounced the *dhimma* covenant. On the last day of the program, one of them wrote this evaluation:

> The results were amazing. Without any exception all those who attended expressed powerfully that this was an essential ministry training topic and a cause for deep blessings and true freedom, especially that everyone had the opportunity to renounce the *dhimma* covenant and declare their covenant with Jesus through his blood. Praise God there is freedom from this pact in the blood of Jesus, through prayer.

A Coptic Christian gained freedom and power to evangelize Muslims

A Coptic Christian lawyer shared this testimony:

> I studied the *sharia* as a major subject for four years as a part of my law degree in an Islamic country. I studied in detail the degradation of Christians under *sharia* law, including the *dhimma* regulations, but something was blocking my understanding of the personal impact of such teachings upon my character. I was a committed Christian and loved the Lord Jesus Christ, but I failed time after time to declare him as my Lord in front of my Muslim friends, lest I hurt their feelings.
>
> When I attended a presentation on dhimmitude I felt that my spiritual condition was being brought into the light, and the deep frustrations in my soul were being exposed. I was remembering many situations when I had happily accepted and even defended the superiority of Muslims in their conquered territory, the land of my ancestors. I became convicted that for many years I had accepted and lived out the degradation of being a *dhimmi*. I sought prayer, and instantly experienced great freedom in Christ.
>
> That same night I went back home and called a close Muslim friend. I told her that Jesus Christ loves her and that he died on the cross for her. Since then my ministry to Muslims has become very effective and I have seen many of them declaring Christ as their Lord and Savior.

Reasons to renounce the *dhimma* covenant

You may wish to pray the declarations and prayers that follow in this lesson for several different reasons:

- You or your ancestors may have lived as non-Muslims under Islamic rule, and accepted a *dhimma* covenant, or have lived under conditions influenced by the principles of *jihad* and dhimmitude.

- Your personal or family history may have been deeply affected by traumatic events, such as experiences of violence associated with jihad or other abuses that can occur under *dhimma* conditions. You may not even have heard of such events, but may suspect that they are a part of your family history.

- You or your ancestors may have been threatened by the Islamic *jihad*, and although there is no family history of actually living under Islam, you wish to be free of the fear and intimidation.

- You or your ancestors may have lived as Muslims and you wish to renounce being a party to the *dhimma* covenant and all its consequences.

These prayers are designed to cancel the *dhimma* covenant, together with all its spiritual consequences, so that it will have no authority over your life. They are also designed to resist and break all curses made against you or your ancestors because of being a *dhimmi* living in an Islamic state. You may also be saying these prayers with a sense of sorrow for lack of knowledge in the past, and wish to stand in the truth of God's Word. They are designed to claim freedom from all the negative spiritual influences of dhimmitude, such as:

- hurt
- fear
- intimidation
- shame
- feelings of guilt
- feelings of inferiority
- self-hatred and self-rejection
- hatred of others
- depression
- deception
- humiliation
- withdrawal and isolation
- silence

We will now consider a prayer to renounce the *dhimma* covenant. This prayer is designed to set Christians free who are living under Islamic dominance today, or whose ancestors have lived under Islamic rule.

Truth encounter

If you have not just done this in the previous lesson, before reciting the prayer to renounce the *dhimma*, read aloud the 'truth encounter' verses in Lesson 5.

This prayer to renounce the *dhimma* is to be read aloud by all participants standing together.

Declaration and Prayer to Renounce the *Dhimma* and Break Its Power

Prayer of confession

Loving God, I confess that I have sinned and turned away from you. I repent and turn to Christ as my Savior and Lord. Please forgive me specifically for any times when I have intimidated others, and sought to impose inferiority or humiliation on others. Forgive me for my pride. Forgive me for any times when I have abused or dominated others. I renounce all these things in Jesus' name.

God and Father of our Lord Jesus Christ, I praise you for the gift of forgiveness won by Christ on the cross. I acknowledge that you have accepted me. I thank you that through the cross we are reconciled to you and to each other. I declare today that I am your child and an inheritor of the Kingdom of God.

Declarations and renunciations

Father, I agree with you that I am not subject to fear, but am a child of your love. I reject and renounce the demands of Islam as taught by Muhammad. I renounce all forms of submission to "Allah of the Quran," and declare that I worship the God of our Lord Jesus Christ alone.

I repent of the sins of my ancestors in submitting to the dhimma covenant and its principles, and ask your forgiveness for their sins.

I renounce and revoke all pacts of surrender made by myself or my ancestors to the community and principles of Islam.

I completely reject the dhimma and every one of its conditions. I renounce the blow on the neck in the jizya payment ritual, together with all that it represents. I specifically renounce the curse of decapitation and death symbolized by this ritual.

I declare that the dhimma covenant is nailed to the cross of Christ. The dhimma has been made a public spectacle, and has no power or rights over me. I declare that the spiritual principles of the dhimma covenant are exposed, disarmed, defeated, and disgraced through the cross of Christ.

I renounce false feelings of gratitude to Islam.

I renounce false feelings of guilt.

I renounce deception and lies.

I renounce all agreements to keep silent about my faith in Christ.

I renounce all agreements to keep silent about the dhimma or Islam.

I will speak and I will not be silent.

I declare that "the truth shall set me free"[13] and I choose to live as a free person in Christ Jesus.

I renounce and cancel all curses spoken against me and my family in the name of Islam. I renounce and cancel all curses spoken against my ancestors.

I specifically renounce and break the curse of death. Death, you have no power over me!

I declare that these curses have no power over me.

I claim the blessings of Christ as my spiritual inheritance.

I renounce intimidation. I choose to be bold in Christ Jesus.

I renounce manipulation and control.

I renounce abuse and violence.

---

13. John 8:32.

I renounce fear. I renounce the fear of being rejected. I renounce the fear of losing my property and possessions. I renounce the fear of poverty. I renounce the fear of being enslaved. I renounce the fear of rape. I renounce the fear of being isolated. I renounce the fear of losing my family. I renounce the fear of being killed and the fear of death.

I renounce the fear of Islam. I renounce the fear of Muslims.

I renounce the fear of being involved in public or political activity.

I declare that Jesus Christ is Lord of all.

I submit to Jesus as Lord of every area of my life. Jesus Christ is Lord of my home. Jesus Christ is Lord of my city. Jesus Christ is Lord of my nation. Jesus Christ is Lord of all peoples in this land. I submit to Jesus Christ as my Lord.

I renounce humiliation. I declare that Christ has accepted me. I serve him and him alone.

I renounce shame. I declare that through the cross I am cleansed from all sin. Shame has no rights over me and I will reign with Christ in glory.

Lord, forgive me and my ancestors for all hatred toward Muslims. I renounce hatred toward Muslims and all others, and declare the love of Christ for Muslims and all other people on this earth.

I repent of the sins of the church and of wrongful submission of church leaders.

I renounce alienation. I declare that I am forgiven and accepted by God through Christ. I am reconciled to God. No power in heaven or on earth can make any charge against me before the throne of God.

I declare my praise and thanks to God our Father, to Christ who is my only Savior, and to the Holy Spirit who alone gives me life.

I commit myself to be a living witness to Jesus Christ as Lord. I am not ashamed of his cross. I am not ashamed of his resurrection.

I declare that I am a child of the living God, the God of Abraham, Isaac, and Jacob.

I declare the victory of God and of his Messiah. I declare that every knee will bow and every tongue confess that Jesus Christ is Lord to the glory of God the Father.

I declare forgiveness toward Muslims for participating in the system of dhimmitude.

Father God, please free me from the dhimma, the spirit of dhimmitude, and every ungodly principle attached to the dhimma covenant.

I ask now that you fill me with your Holy Spirit, and pour upon me all the blessings of the kingdom of Jesus Christ. Grant me grace to understand the truth of your Word clearly and apply it in every area of my life. Grant to me words of hope and life, as you promised you would, and bless my lips so I can speak them to others with authority and power in Jesus' name. Give me the boldness to be a faithful witness to Christ. Grant me a deep love for Muslim people and a passion to share the love of Christ with them.

I declare and ask these things in the name of Jesus Christ my Lord and Savior.

Amen.

Study Guide

Lesson 6

Vocabulary

dhimma	*jizya*	dhimmitude
dhimmi	*wajib*	ritual of decapitation
Regensburg lecture	*jihad*	truth encounter
'three choices'	Pact of Umar	
Grand Mufti	*halal*	

New names

- Pope Benedict XVI (b. 1927): German born Joseph Ratzinger, Pope from 2005-2013
- Byzantine Emperor Manuel II Palaeologus (1350-1425; ruled 1395-1425)
- Sheikh Abdul Aziz al-Sheikh: Grand Mufti in Saudi Arabia since 1999 (born 1943)
- Ibn Kathir: Syrian historian and scholar (1301-1373)
- Muhammad ibn Yusuf Atfayyish: Algerian Muslim scholar (1818-1914)
- William Eton: British researcher in Turkey and Russia, published *Survey of the Turkish Empire* in 1798
- Ibn Qudama: Palestinian Sunni scholar and Sufi mystic (1147-1223)
- Samuel ha-Nagid (993-1055/56) and Joseph ha-Nagid (1035-1066): Jewish Grand Viziers in Granada.
- Muhammad al-Maghili: Algerian scholar (c. 1400-c. 1505)
- Ibn Ajibah: Moroccan Sunni Sufi scholar (1747-1809)
- Maimonides: Iberian Sephardic Jewish scholar (1138-1204)
- Jovan Cvijic: Serbian geographer and ethnologist (1865-1927)

Quran in this lesson

Q9:29   Q48:28   Q3:110

Questions Lesson 6

- Discuss the case study.

The *dhimma* covenant

1. What famous words did Byzantine Emperor **Manuel II Palaeologus** declare which **Pope Benedict** XVI quoted in his famous 2006 **Regensburg lecture**, and which caused Muslims to riot worldwide, leading to some 100 fatalities?

2. What correction did **Grand Mufti Sheikh Abdul Aziz al-Sheikh** give to Pope Benedict?

3. What are the **three choices** that Islam offers non-Muslims when they are conquered?

4. Durie quotes a *hadith* from *Sahih al-Bukhari* ("I have been ordered …"). What is Allah's order according to this quote?

5. Durie next quotes a *hadith* from *Sahih Muslim*: "Fight in the name of Allah and in the way of Allah. Fight against those who disbelieve …" From what three choices are the conquered disbelievers in Islam invited to choose?

6. What two things does Q9:29 require of conquered non-Muslims?

7. What is the name of the pact that is a covenant of surrender?

8. What are non-Muslims called who accept to live under this pact?

9. What two quranic principles uphold the **dhimma** system?

Jizya

10. Why is the annual *jizya* tax on the **dhimmis** spoken of by Muslim scholars as a redemption for their blood?

11. For whose benefit, says Imam **Atfayyish**, is the substitution of *jizya* tax for killing and slavery?

12. According to **William Eton**, for what is the *jizya* a compensation?

The penalty for non-compliance

13. What awaited the **dhimmis** if they were not compliant with the **dhimma** covenant?

14. What did the **Pact of Umar** require *dhimmis* to invoke upon themselves?

15. What did Imam **Ibn Qudama** mean by making the disobedient *dhimmi* person and goods *halal* 'licit'?

16. What traumatic events have occurred in the history of *dhimmi* communities?

17. Why were the Jews of Granada killed in 1066?

18. Why were Christians massacred in Damascus in 1860? What did some do to avoid being killed?

A disturbing ritual

19. What was the ritual that Durie says was widespread from Morocco to Bukhara for more than one thousand years?

20. What meaning is this ritual intended to express?

21. What curse was invoked by a *dhimmi* when he went through this ritual?

22. What do participants invoke against themselves when they enact the payment of the *jizya* tax?

23. What does the *dhimmi* pronounce upon himself in paying the *jizya* tax?

Humble gratitude

24. According to Durie, what are the two attitudes that non-Muslims are to adopt toward Muslims?

25. Note the examples of inferiority imposed by *sharia* regulations on non-Muslims:

- *Dhimmis'* witness
- *Dhimmis'* houses
- *Dhimmis'* horses
- *Dhimmis'* walking on a public road
- *Dhimmis'* self-defense
- *Dhimmis'* religious symbols
- *Dhimmis'* churches
- *Dhimmis'* criticism of Islam
- *Dhimmis'* dress
- *Dhimmis'* marriages

26. What does Q9:29 command of non-Muslims living under Muslim rule?

27. How did **Ibn Ajibah** describe the 'third choice'?

A psychology of inferiority

28. What does the term '**dhimmitude**' describe?

29. What does **dhimmitude** cause *dhimmis* to do, according to the medieval Iberian Jewish scholar, Maimonides?

30. According to Serbian geographer **Jovan Cvijic**, what did the violent **dhimmitude** enforced by the Turks upon the Balkan population psychologically produce?

31. According to one Iranian convert to Christianity who spoke to Mark Durie, how do Muslims perceive their own religion in relation to Christianity?

32. Why does **dhimmitude** also damage Muslims?

33. To what historic situation in the United States of America does Durie compare **dhimmitude**?

34. What, according to Durie, is crippling academic inquiry and political discourse?

Religious persecution and the *dhimma's* return

35. What forced the Muslim world to dismantle the *dhimma* system in the nineteenth and twentieth centuries?

36. According to Durie, what has caused growing persecution of Christians in Pakistan and is also causing the growing persecution of Christians in many other nations?

A spiritual solution

37. What five spiritual consequences of Muhammad's deep experience of rejection does Durie list?

38. What was the root that drove Muhammad's call for *jihad*?

39. What four things did Christ refuse to do when he was rejected?

Testimonies of freedom from the *dhimma*

40. What do these five testimonies that Durie shares have in common?

Reasons to renounce the *dhimma* covenant

41. Which three influences may affect someone seeking prayer for either having lived under or having ancestors who lived under **dhimmitude**?

42. What two things are the prayers concerning **dhimmitude** designed to do?

43. Look at the list of 13 negative spiritual influences caused by **dhimmitude**. What will prayers based upon the truth of God's Word do to these influences?

For the prayers section, please follow the following steps:

1. The **truth encounter** verses in Lesson 5 are read out aloud to all participants, if they have not already been read when doing that lesson.

2. After this, all participants stand together and recite the 'Declaration and Prayer to Renounce the *Dhimma* and Break Its Power'.

3. For more detailed instructions, see the Guide for Leaders.

7

Lying, False Superiority, and Cursing

"The tongue has the power of life and death,
and those who love it will eat its fruit."
Proverbs 18:21

Lesson objectives

a. Consider and reject Islam's permission to lie and deceive others.

b. Consider scriptural verses declaring 20 specific truths as you prepare to renounce Islamic deception.

c. Claim spiritual freedom from deception by reciting a prayer of renunciation, including eight unique declarations and renunciations.

d. Consider and reject Islam's quest for the superiority of one person over another.

e. Consider scriptural verses declaring specific truths as you prepare to renounce Islamic superiority.

f. Claim spiritual freedom from false superiority by reciting a prayer of renunciation, including 11 unique declarations and renunciations.

g. Consider Islamic ritual practices of large numbers of worshippers cursing disbelievers together at the mosque.

h. Note the varying attitudes to cursing in Islam.

i. Note the emotional connection and 'charge' that participants in ritual cursing can feel.

j. Consider scriptural verses declaring six specific truths as you prepare to renounce ritual cursing.

k. Claim spiritual freedom from cursing rituals by reciting a prayer of renunciation, including 19 unique declarations and renunciations.

Case study: What would you do?

You are on a journey in a church minibus with three Christian colleagues named Alexander, Samuel, and Pierre. You are traveling to a conference addressing discipleship among Muslims. After sharing about church, family, and politics, Pierre asks what others think about the many dreams Muslims are having of Christ and the rise of militant Islam. Does this mean we are in the last times? Should converted Muslims deserve a special path of discipleship, like Jews who follow Jesus as Messiah?

Alexander says cynically, "Seriously men, why do converted Muslims need any different discipleship from, say, Jews, or Buddhists? When has the historic church offered different discipleship for different religious backgrounds? Don't we all use the same Bible and recite the same creed? What evidence is there that Muslims are 'born again' differently and need special baptismal teaching or discipleship?"

Samuel replies, "Jesus promised every knee would bow, and I believe this includes millions of Muslims coming to Christ, and we must welcome them with special attention, in special household churches, as we do with Jews. Both Paul and Peter treated evangelism to the Jews differently from evangelism to the Gentiles. We should treat Muslims like 'Jewish cousins' and have a special discipleship that addresses their spiritual needs."

Pierre then adds, "But Samuel, all the apostles used the same doctrines to disciple the New Testament church. Are not all of the apostolic epistles addressed to both Jews and Gentiles? Muslims coming to Christ simply need what everyone else needs: a baptismal course, sermons, Sunday School teaching, and Bible studies. In fact, giving them special treatment could keep them from integrating into our existing churches."

Samuel next says to you, "How do you see discipleship for former Muslims?"

How will you answer?

Freedom from lying

In these sections we will consider the teaching of Islam concerning lying, and we will choose to renounce lies.

Truth is precious

Pastor Damanik, who was falsely imprisoned in Indonesia for speaking up against the Islamic *jihad*, said this about truth:

> … although truth is difficult and very expensive we don't have any choice. We have to be willing to pay the expensive price. The alternative is to say goodbye to the truth. The truth lover has to fight extra hard to be someone with an iron will and at the same time be a person with a pure and transparent heart (like glass). The iron will is strong; it cannot be bent. It is unswerving in its commitment to truth … The glass heart is one that is clean from one's own hidden interests and personal agenda. As with glass, the truth lover is sensitive and easily broken over the injustice and falsehood in the world. This broken-heartedness is not a sign of weakness, but it is a sign of strength and power. He is strong willed and his sharp mouth is able to speak out in the face of untruth and the falsehood of his surroundings. His heart cannot be still or quiet. His heart is always full of fight against injustice.

The fact that God is truthful is fundamental for us in entering into relationship with him. God is relational: he binds himself into relationships with humanity.

Sharia culture

According to the Quran and the teachings of Islam, lying is permitted under certain circumstances. We have seen in Lesson 3 how lying is permitted and sometimes obligatory in Islam.

In the Quran even Allah is said to be deceptive, leading people astray:

Allah leads astray whomever he pleases, and he guides whomever he pleases. He is the Mighty, the Wise. (Q14:4)

Types of lies that *sharia* law endorses include:

- lying in warfare
- husbands lying to wives
- lying to protect oneself
- lying to defend the *Umma*
- self-protective lying (*taqiyya*) when Muslims believe they are in danger: in this case a Muslim is even permitted to deny their faith (Q16:106).

These religious values have influenced Islamic cultures in deep ways.

Truth encounter

Unlike in Islam, a Christian is not permitted to deny their faith:

Whoever acknowledges me before others, I will also acknowledge before my Father in heaven. But whoever disowns me before others, I will disown before my Father in heaven. (Matthew 10:32-33)

Jesus said, "All you need to say is simply 'Yes' or 'No' …" (Matthew 5:37)

According to Genesis 17, what does God establish with Abraham?

I will establish my covenant as an everlasting covenant between me and you and your descendants after you for the generations to come, to be your God and the God of your descendants after you. The whole land of Canaan, where you are now an alien, I will give as an everlasting possession to you and your descendants after you; and I will be their God. (Genesis 17:7-8)

And according to Psalm 89, what does God establish with David?

You said, "I have made a covenant with my chosen one, I have sworn to David my servant, 'I will establish your line forever and make your throne firm through all generations.'" (Psalm 89:3-4)

These two passages you have just read show that God establishes faithful covenants with his people.

What two relationship attributes of God can you discern in these next passages?

> God is not human, that he should lie, nor a human being, that he should change his mind. Does he speak and then not act? Does he promise and not fulfill? (Numbers 23:19)

> Give thanks to the Lord for he is good. His love endures forever. (Psalm 136:1)

> [speaking of the Jews] ... as far as election is concerned, they are loved on account of the patriarchs, for God's gifts and his call are irrevocable. (Romans 11:28-29)

> ... the faith of God's elect and their knowledge of the truth that leads to godliness—in the hope of eternal life, which God, who does not lie, promised before the beginning of time ... (Titus 1:1-2)

> Because God wanted to make the unchanging nature of his purpose very clear to the heirs of what was promised, he confirmed it with an oath. God did this so that, by two unchangeable things in which it is impossible for God to lie, we who have fled to take hold of the hope offered to us may be greatly encouraged. We have this hope as an anchor for the soul, firm and secure. (Hebrews 6:17-19)

> But as surely as God is faithful, our message to you is not "Yes" and "No." For the Son of God, Jesus Christ ... was not "Yes" and "No," but in him it has always been "Yes." (2 Corinthians 1:18-20)

God is unchanging and faithful in his relationships. He always keeps his word.

According to Leviticus, what does God want of people?

> The Lord said to Moses, "Speak to the entire assembly of Israel and say to them: 'Be holy because I, the Lord your God, am holy.'" (Leviticus 19:1-2)

The true God of the Bible wants us to be holy like him.

According to these next three verses, how do we show God's holiness in our lives?

> ... for I have always been mindful of your unfailing love and have lived in reliance on your truth.[14] (Psalm 26:3)

> Into your hands I commit my spirit; deliver me, Lord, my faithful God. (Psalm 31:5)

> Do not withhold your mercy from me, O Lord; may your love and your truth always protect me. (Psalm 40:11)

We can show God's holiness by being truthful, and living in truth, because God is true and faithful to his word. Although Satan loves to put lies into our hearts, God's truth protects us.

What does truth do to us, according to this Psalm of David?

> Surely I was sinful at birth; sinful from the time my mother conceived me.
> Surely you desired truth even in the womb; you teach me wisdom in the inmost place.
> Cleanse me with hyssop, and I will be clean; wash me, and I will be whiter than snow. (Psalm 51:5-7)

This Psalm states that truth cleanses us.

According to this verse, what filled Jesus' life?

> ... we have seen his glory, the glory as of a father's only Son, full of grace and truth. (John 1:14)

Jesus was full of truth.

In what are we called to live?

> But those who do what is true come to the light, so that it may be clearly seen that their deeds have been done in God. (John 3:21)

We are called to live in truth.

According to these next two verses, through what alone can we come to know God?

---

14. The word translated 'truth' here can also mean 'faithfulness'.

God is spirit, and his worshipers must worship in spirit and in truth. (John 4:24)

Jesus answered, "I am the way, and the truth, and the life. No one comes to the Father except through me." (John 14:6)

Jesus is telling us that we can only come to God through truth. (In the Gospels, Jesus says "I tell you the truth" 78 times.)

What is incompatible with following Christ, according to this passage from Paul?

We also know that law is made not for the righteous but for lawbreakers and rebels, the ungodly and sinful, the unholy and irreligious; for those who kill their fathers or mothers, for murderers, for adulterers and perverts, for slave traders and liars and perjurers—and for whatever else is contrary to the sound doctrine that conforms to the glorious gospel of the blessed God, which he entrusted to me. (1 Timothy 1:9-11)

Paul is explaining that lying is incompatible with following Christ.

This prayer to renounce deception is to be read aloud by all participants standing together.

Declaration and Prayer to Renounce Deception

I thank you Father that you are a God of truth, that you shine your light into the darkest night. Today I choose not to live in darkness, but to dwell in your light.

Please forgive me for all the lies I have spoken. I have so often chosen the path of comfort and what is easy, not what is right. I ask you Lord to cleanse my lips from all ungodliness. Give me a heart that delights to hear the truth, and a mouth ready to make the truth known to others.

Give me courage to take comfort in the truth, and to reject the lies.

Today I reject and renounce the use of lies in my everyday life.

I reject all the teachings of Islam that are used to justify telling lies, including taqiyya. I choose to turn away from all lying and deception. I choose to live in the truth.

I declare that Jesus Christ is the way, the truth, and the life. I choose to live under the protection of his truth.

I declare that my security is in you, and the truth shall set me free.

Please show me, heavenly Father, how to walk in the light of your truth. Give me the words to speak, and a way to walk in, which is based upon your truth.

Amen.

Freedom from false superiority

In this section we consider Islam's teachings on the superiority of some people over others, and we contrast this with the teachings of the Bible. Then we will choose to renounce feelings of false superiority.

Islam's claim to superiority

In Islam there is a great emphasis on superiority; on who is 'the best'. The Quran says that Muslims are better than Christians and Jews:

> You [Muslims] are the best community brought forth for humankind, commanding right and forbidding wrong, and believing in God. If the People of the Book had believed, it would have been better for them; some of them are believers, but most of them are wicked. (Q3:110)

And Islam is supposed to rule over other religions:

> It is he who has sent his messenger with the guidance and the religion of truth, that he may cause it to prevail over every religion. (Q48:28)

In Islam it is shameful to be regarded as inferior. There are many *hadiths* of Muhammad that place a great emphasis on superiority. For example, Muhammad declared in a *hadith* reported by al-Timirdhi that he was superior to all other people who have ever lived:

> I will be the master of the children of Adam on the Day of Judgment, and I am not boasting. The banner of praise will be

in my hand, and I am not boasting. On that day every prophet, including Adam, will be under my banner. And I am the first one for whom the earth will be opened [i.e. the first to be resurrected] and I am not boasting.

The religion of Islam has had a deep influence on Arabic culture, shaping it over more than a thousand years. In Arabic cultures, concepts of honor and shame are very important, so people hate to be made to seem inferior. When people are in conflict they can try to humiliate each other and they will act out of a sense of offense.

When someone leaves Islam and decides to follow Christ, they must renounce the emotional worldview in which a person needs to feel superior to those around them, gains satisfaction from this, and fears being shamed.

Truth encounter

In the Garden of Eden, the snake tempted Eve by telling her she could become "like God," and on this basis Eve went along with what the snake wanted. This led to the Fall of Adam and Eve. What can we learn from this passage about the danger of desiring to be superior?

> The woman said to the serpent, "We may eat fruit from the trees in the garden, but God did say, 'You must not eat fruit from the tree that is in the middle of the garden, and you must not touch it, or you will die.'"
>
> "You will not certainly die," the serpent said to the woman. "For God knows that when you eat from it your eyes will be opened, and you will be like God, knowing good and evil." (Genesis 3:2-5)

The desire to be superior is a trap for human beings: a great deal of trouble and pain can be caused in this world by people wanting to be superior to others.

From time to time a question came up among Jesus' followers as to who was or would be the best among them. James and John wanted to know who would have the place of honor in Jesus' kingdom. Like James and John, human beings all over the world seek the best seats or the places of greatest honor. What does Jesus have to say about this?

Then James and John, the sons of Zebedee, came to him. "Teacher," they said, "we want you to do for us whatever we ask."

"What do you want me to do for you?" he asked.

They replied, "Let one of us sit at your right and the other at your left in your glory." ...

When the ten heard about this, they became indignant with James and John. Jesus called them together and said, "You know that those who are regarded as rulers of the Gentiles[15] lord it over them, and their high officials exercise authority over them. Not so with you. Instead, whoever wants to become great among you must be your servant, and whoever wants to be first must be slave of all. For even the Son of Man did not come to be served, but to serve, and to give his life as a ransom for many." (Mark 10:35-45)

Jesus responds to this desire by explaining that if his disciples truly want to follow him, they have to learn how to serve others.

The danger of feeling superior also comes out in the story of the prodigal son (Luke 15:11-32). The 'good' son felt himself to be superior and was unable to join his father's party for the long-lost son when he returned. For this he was rebuked by his father. The pathway to real success, in God's eyes, is to seek to serve others, not to look down on them or lord it over them.

In this beautiful passage from Philippians 2, what is the key to being set free from the oppression of seeing the world in terms of superiority of some people over others?

Therefore if you have any encouragement from being united with Christ, if any comfort from his love, if any common sharing in the Spirit, if any tenderness and compassion, then make my joy complete by being like-minded, having the same love, being one in spirit and of one mind. Do nothing out of selfish ambition or vain conceit. Rather, in humility value others

15. When Jesus refers here to the Gentiles, he means all the nations: it is a universal trait of human nature to want to feel important.

above yourselves, not looking to your own interests but each of you to the interests of the others.

In your relationships with one another, have the same mindset as Christ Jesus: Who, being in very nature God, did not consider equality with God something to be used to his own advantage; rather, he made himself nothing by taking the very nature of a servant, being made in human likeness.

And being found in appearance as a man, he humbled himself by becoming obedient to death—even death on a cross!

Therefore God exalted him to the highest place and gave him the name that is above every name, that at the name of Jesus every knee should bow, in heaven and on earth and under the earth, and every tongue acknowledge that Jesus Christ is Lord, to the glory of God the Father. (Philippians 2:1-11)

The key to being released from an oppressive worldview of superiority is the example of Jesus Christ.

The heart of Jesus is quite different. He chose to serve, not to dominate. He did not kill, but offered his life for others. In very practical ways, Jesus showed what it meant to humble yourself: he "made himself nothing" (Philippians 2:7), even allowing himself to be crucified, the most disgraceful death known to people in his time.

The true follower of Christ does the same. He or she gains no pleasure from any sense of feeling superior. True Christ-followers are not afraid of shame or what other people think, because they trust in God to vindicate and protect them.

This prayer to renounce a false sense of superiority is to be read aloud by all participants standing together.

Declaration and Prayer to Renounce Superiority

I thank you, Father, that I am wonderfully made, because it is you who made me. Thank you that you love me and call me your own. Thank you for the privilege of following Jesus Christ.

Please forgive me for accepting the desire to feel superior. I renounce and utterly reject such desires. I refuse to take comfort in feeling better than others. I acknowledge that I am a sinner, like everyone else, and I can accomplish nothing without you.

I also repent of and renounce feelings of belonging to a superior group or background. I confess that all peoples are equal in your sight.

I repent of uttering words of contempt for others and rejection of others, and seek your forgiveness for all these words.

I reject thinking less of people because of their race, their gender, their wealth, or their education.

I acknowledge that it is only by the grace of God that I can stand in your presence. I separate myself from all human judgment, and look to you alone to save me.

I specifically renounce Islam's teaching that the righteous are superior, that Islam makes people successful, and that Muslims are superior to non-Muslims.

I reject and renounce the claim that men are superior to women.

Heavenly Father, I turn away from every false sense of superiority and instead I choose to serve you.

Lord, I also choose to rejoice in the successes of others. I reject and renounce all envy and jealousy of others.

Lord, please give me a sound and accurate judgment about who I am in you. Teach me the truth of how you see me. Help me to be content as the person you have created me to be.

Amen.

Freedom from cursing

In these sections we consider the practice of cursing others in Islam, choose to renounce this practice, and break any curses that have been made against us.

Cursing in Islam

Using the resources in Lesson 2, believers can develop prayer strategies to help people be set free from many different kinds of bondages, whether from Islam or other sources.

In this section we consider a particular Islamic ritual and provide a prayer to renounce it. This prayer was developed because a Christian from a Muslim background mentioned to me that this ritual had been a significant part of his religious experience as a Muslim, and it was one that he felt had spiritual power.

The Quran urges the cursing of Christians who confess the deity of Christ: "Let us humbly pray and invoke Allah's curse upon the liars" (Q3:61). However, the *hadiths* have conflicting statements about cursing. On one hand, several *hadiths* report Muhammad cursing various categories of people, including Jews or Christians, and men or women who imitate the opposite sex. On the other hand, there are *hadiths* that warn against the dangers of cursing, and say that Muslims should never curse a fellow Muslim.

Because of these conflicting accounts, Muslim scholars have different opinions about whether it is legitimate for Muslims to curse others, who they can curse, and what is the Islamic way to do it. Yet cursing of non-Muslims is very common in Islamic cultures. In 1836 Edward Lane wrote that Muslim school children in Egypt were being taught curses to recite against Christians, Jews, and all other unbelievers in Islam.[16]

Ritual cursing

I have spoken with former Muslims from different countries who said it was their custom to attend mass cursing events at the mosque.

One friend described these events, which were led by the imam of the mosque, who is the official who leads the Friday prayers. The men would form up in lines "shoulder to shoulder." Following the imam, and reciting altogether, they would curse those they considered to be enemies of Islam. The curses were ritualistic and repetitive. This

---

16. Edward W. Lane, *An Account of the Manners and Customs of the Modern Egyptians*, p. 276.

friend said that the cursers would experience an emotional high, a very strong feeling of hatred and excitement, with an intense spiritual "charge" (a feeling of power flowing through their bodies). This practice, in his experience, was passed on from father to son and it bonded them together. It made him feel connected to his father, and through him to his grandfather, and other ancestors before that: they had all stood "shoulder to shoulder" to curse others for the sake of Islam.

Another friend from Saudi Arabia, now a Christian, used to look forward to a certain day in Ramadan, the fasting month, when thousands of men would gather at the Great Mosque of Mecca to pray together. He always looked forward with excitement to the moment when non-Muslims would be cursed by the multitude. He too experienced that spiritual "charge" as he joined in the curses. The imam would be weeping as he called down curses upon the infidels, and everyone present would focus their energy and hatred into that moment, supporting the imam's cursing words.

Such an event conflicts with Jesus' teaching that cursing is forbidden (Luke 6:28): Christians are taught not to curse others, but to return blessings for curses. Such a ritual also establishes an ungodly 'soul tie' between a worshipper and the imam, as well as between father and son when they do it together. These experiences of cursing had a big impact on my friend when he was younger, before he got to know Jesus.

What does the expression 'soul tie' mean? It means one person's soul is connected to another's: they are not free of each other. A soul tie is a kind of open door or foothold, one which we did not discuss in Lesson 2. In essence, a soul tie is a covenant that binds two people together so spiritual influence can pass from one to the other. Some soul ties can be good and indeed can be a source of blessing, such as a godly soul tie between a parent and child, but others can be a source of harm.

When someone has an ungodly soul tie, forgiveness is important to make sure the soul tie is cut. As long as someone holds unforgiveness against someone else, there is still an ungodly bond or link—a soul tie—between them.

Soul ties can be ungodly. Fortunately, Christians can cut or break ungodly soul ties, removing them using the five-step process described in Lesson 2: confession, renouncing, breaking, casting out (when required), and finally blessing.

How to break a curse

I was teaching at a conference when a young man approached me to ask for help. He and his family had moved to a Middle Eastern country where he was being trained to serve as a missionary. However, the family was experiencing many difficulties including accidents and sicknesses. The circumstances had become so bad that they were thinking about giving up and going home. The young man wondered whether their apartment might be cursed but he did not know what to do about it. I shared with him how to break a curse. He then took this advice back home and took authority to pray through his apartment, breaking all curses. After this, the family's difficulties went away, and they were able to enjoy their home in peace.

Many involved in ministry to Muslims, including Believers from Muslim Backgrounds, have been subjected to curses by Muslims. These could be curses done in the name of Allah or using witchcraft.

If you believe you or someone you love may have been cursed, here are nine steps to take to remove the curse:

- First, confess and repent of all sin and declare the covering of the blood of Jesus over your life.

- Then remove any ungodly or dedicated objects from your home.

- Next, forgive whoever has generated the curse, including yourself, whether by sin or by someone's deliberate act of cursing.

- Recognize and claim the authority you have in Christ.

- Renounce and break the curse, saying "*I renounce and break this curse in the name of Jesus*," claiming the sovereign power and authority of Jesus Christ over every work of darkness, by his cross.

- Declare your freedom from all evil in Christ, because of Christ's finished work on the cross.

- Command any and every demon associated with the curse to leave you, your family, and your home.

- Then declare blessings over yourself, your family and your home, including the opposite of any curse, using Bible verses where fitting, such as, "I will not die but live, and will proclaim what the Lord has done." (Psalm 118:17)

- Praise God for his love, power, and grace.

Truth encounter

What does this verse say about how are we set free from curses?

> In him we have redemption through his blood, the forgiveness of sins, in accordance with the riches of God's grace ... (Ephesians 1:7)

We are set free from curses because we are redeemed by the blood of Christ.

What authority does a Christian have over the power of evil?

> "Behold, I give you the authority to trample on serpents and scorpions, and over all the power of the enemy, and nothing shall by any means hurt you." (Luke 10:19)

We must recognize that in Christ we can take authority over all the power of the enemy, including over all curses.

According to this next verse, why did Jesus come to this world?

> The reason the Son of God appeared was to destroy the devil's work. (1 John 3:8)

Jesus came to destroy the power of Satan, including all evil curses.

How did Jesus' crucifixion fulfill the law of Deuteronomy 21:23?

> Christ redeemed us from the curse of the law by becoming a curse for us, for it is written: "Cursed is everyone who is hung on a pole." He redeemed us in order that the blessing given to Abraham might come to the Gentiles through Christ Jesus, so

that by faith we might receive the promise of the Spirit. (Galatians 3:13-14)

In Deuteronomy 21:23 it says that anyone who hangs on a pole or tree is cursed. Jesus Christ was cursed in this way, being put to death on a cross, so that we could be set free from curses. He bore the curse for us, so that we might receive blessing.

What does this verse say about an undeserved curse?

Like a fluttering sparrow or a darting swallow, an undeserved curse does not come to rest. (Proverbs 26:2)

This verse reminds us that we are protected and free from curses when we claim the protection of the blood and the freedom of the cross, and apply them to our situation.

What does this next verse say about the power of the blood over curses?

But you have come to Mount Zion ... You have come to ... Jesus the mediator of a new covenant, and to the sprinkled blood that speaks a better word than the blood of Abel. (Hebrews 12:24)

The blood of Jesus speaks a better word than the curse of Cain, shed by his brother Abel. The blood also speaks a better word than curses we have been subjected to.

What positive command and example is given to Christians in Luke 6, and in Paul's letters?

I say, "Love your enemies, do good to those who hate you, bless those who curse you, pray for those who mistreat you." (Luke 6:27-28)

Bless those you persecute you; bless and do not curse. (Romans 12:14)

We work hard with our own hands. When we are cursed, we bless; when we are persecuted, we endure it ... (1 Corinthians 4:12)

Christians are called to be people of blessing, whether for friends or for enemies.

This is a prayer to be set free from the effects of participating in cursing rituals, and also to be set free from curses sent by others. It applies the principles developed in Lesson 2.

Declaration and Prayer to Renounce Cursing

I confess the sins of my ancestors and my parents and my own sins of cursing others in the name of Islam.

I choose to forgive and release my ancestors, my father, the imams who led them and me in these curses, and all others who have influenced me to commit this sin, and for the consequences in my life.

I choose to forgive all who have cursed me or my family.

I ask you to forgive me, Lord, for yielding to and participating in the cursing of others.

I receive your forgiveness now.

On the basis of your forgiveness, Lord, I choose to forgive myself for cursing others.

I renounce the sin of cursing, and any curses that have resulted from this sin.

I renounce the hatred of others.

I renounce the intense emotion of participating in cursing others.

I break these powers from my life (and from the lives of my descendants) through the redemptive work of Christ on the cross.

I ask you, Lord, to break all curses I have participated in, and to bless those I have cursed with all the blessings of the Kingdom of God.

In the name of Jesus, I also renounce and break all curses made against me.

I reject and renounce all demons of hatred and cursing, and command them to leave me now, in the name of Jesus.

I receive God's freedom from all curses against me and my family. I receive peace, gentleness, and authority to bless others.

I consecrate my lips to speak words of praise and blessing all my days.

In the name of Jesus, I declare the full blessings of the Kingdom of God over myself and my family, including life, good health, and joy.

I confess and renounce all ungodly connections, soul ties, and attachments with imams and other Muslim leaders who have led me in Islamic rituals, including cursing of others.

I forgive these leaders for their part in establishing or maintaining my ungodly soul ties.

I forgive myself for my part in maintaining these ungodly soul ties with all Muslims whose leadership I have submitted to.

I ask you Lord, to forgive me for every sin associated with establishing or maintaining these soul ties, especially the sins of cursing others and hating others.

I now break all ungodly soul ties and attachments to Muslim leaders [specifically naming any particular ones that come to mind] and release myself from them [or name] and them [or name] from me.

Lord, please cleanse my mind from all memories of ungodly unions so I am free to give myself to you.

I renounce and cancel the assignments of all demons attempting to maintain these ungodly soul ties, and command them to leave me now, in the name of Jesus.

I bind myself to Christ Jesus and choose to follow only him.

Amen.

Study Guide

Lesson 7

Vocabulary

taqiyya   *imam*   soul ties

New names

- Rinaldy Damanik: Indonesian pastor (born 1957)

Bible in this lesson

Matthew 10:32-33   John 4:24

Matthew 5:37   John 14:6

Genesis 17:7-8   1 Timothy 1:9-11

Psalm 89:3-4   Genesis 3:2-5

Numbers 23:19   Mark 10:35-45

Psalm 136:1   Luke 15:11-32

Romans 11:28-29   Philippians 2:1-11

Titus 1:1-2   Luke 6:28

Hebrews 6:17-19   Psalm 118:17

2 Corinthians 1:18-20   Ephesians 1:7

Leviticus 19:1-2   1 John 3:8

Psalm 26:3   Deuteronomy 21:23

Psalm 31:5   Galatians 3:13-14

Psalm 40:11	Proverbs 26:2
Psalm 51:5-7	Luke 6:27-28
John 1:14	Romans 12:14
John 3:21	1 Corinthians 4:12

Quran in this lesson

Q14:4   Q16:106   Q3:110   Q48:28   Q3:61

Questions Lesson 7

- Discuss the case study.

Freedom from lying

Truth is precious

1. For which scriptural conviction was **Pastor Damanik** willing to go to jail?

2. Why does God bind himself into relationships with humanity?

Sharia culture

3. What does Durie point out is permitted in the Quran?

4. According to Q14:4, how does Allah lead people?

5. What are some forms of lying that are permitted in *sharia* law?

6. What is permitted to Muslims Q16:106 but not (according to Matthew 10:28-33) to Christians?

Truth encounter

The 'truth encounter' verses are read to all participants.

The prayer

After the 'truth encounter' verses have been read to the whole group, all participants stand and say the 'Declaration and Prayer to Renounce Deception' together.

Freedom from false superiority

Islam's claim to superiority

7. What is promised to Muslims in the Quran according to Q3:110 and Q48:28?

8. Who claimed to be the most superior person who ever lived?

9. What concepts are very important in the Arab culture?

10. What also needs to be renounced when someone leaves Islam?

Truth encounter

The 'truth encounter' verses are read to all participants.

The prayer

After the truth encounter verses have been read to the whole group, all participants stand and say the 'Declaration and Prayer to Renounce Superiority' together.

Freedom from cursing

Cursing in Islam

11. Why do Muslim scholars have different opinions about cursing in Islam?

12. According to Edward Lane, what were Muslim school children in Egypt being taught to do in 1836?

Ritual cursing

13. Durie reports a ritual that a Christian from a Muslim background used to take part in. How did taking part in this ritual make him feel?

14. How does Durie define a **soul tie**?

15. How is forgiveness important in dealing with **soul ties**?

16. Consider the 'Declaration and Prayer to Renounce Cursing'. Can you identify the points where these five steps are applied: confession, renouncing, breaking, casting out, and blessing? (See Lesson 2.)

17. What things are renounced and what are broken in this prayer?

18. What blessings are claimed instead of curses? Why these particular blessings?

19. Who is forgiven in this prayer?

How to break a curse

20. What did the young man who spoke to Mark Durie think might be causing his family's problems?

21. Why couldn't he fix this problem by himself?

22. What did the young man need to do before he could live in peace?

23. What causes difficulties for many people involved in ministry to Muslims?

24. What are the nine steps Durie suggests for breaking a curse?

Truth encounter

The 'truth encounter' verses are read to all participants.

The prayer

After the 'truth encounter' verses have been read to the whole group, all participants stand and say the 'Declaration and Prayer to Renounce Cursing' together.

8

A Free Church

"If you abide in me and I in you, you will bear much fruit."
John 15:5

Lesson objectives

a. Appreciate the different kinds of difficulties faced by Believers from a Muslim Background in becoming mature disciples with a mature faith.

b. Understand that it is not enough to lead someone to Christ: they also need to be brought to Christian maturity.

c. Consider the importance of a healthy church in forming healthy disciples.

d. Appreciate that to stay free, the believer must close all doors to the enemy, and be filled with the good things of Jesus Christ.

e. Appreciate the role of the church in helping believers do this.

f. Understand the importance of ministering freedom, not just in areas due to Islam.

g. Learn to be intentional about 'teaching into the gaps' to strengthen disciples specifically in the areas in which Islam has caused weaknesses.

h. Value a strong start to the Christian life, including a renunciation of agreements with Islam and a full transfer of one's allegiance to Christ as Lord.

i. Consider the value of a thorough believer's prayer.

j. Appreciate the importance of mentoring leaders who have converted from Islam.

k. Consider some key aspects in forming leaders.

Case study: What would you do?

You are an experienced pastor who has led several successful churches and you are well known for giving wise advice to other pastors. You are visiting a relative in another city and someone has asked you to make contact with his good friend Reza, an Iranian church leader, while you are there. Reza leads a congregation of around 100 Iranian converts from Islam, but you are told that his church is in trouble: there is a lot of conflict, some key members have recently left after accusing him of acting like a dictator, giving is going down, and the church can no longer afford to pay the pastor's salary. You make contact with Pastor Reza, pass on your contact's greetings, and after chatting over a coffee for a while, you ask him how things are going in his church. He says, "Excellent! Everything is excellent, praise God."

How will you respond?

───────

This lesson offers suggestions for how to support a healthy discipleship path and build a healthy church environment for Believers from a Muslim Background (BMBs): people who have chosen to leave Islam to follow Christ. It is good for every disciple to desire to be ready and suitable to serve God's special purposes (2 Timothy 2:20-21) but to achieve this, everyone needs a healthy church environment which can support their growth. Before considering how to achieve this, we will first consider three challenges faced by converts: falling away to return to Islam, unfruitful discipleship, and unhealthy churches.

Falling away

Some people who leave Islam to follow Christ end up going back to Islam. There are many reasons for this. One reason can be the pain of loss of community, when Muslim family and friends reject a convert to Christianity. Another reason is the many obstacles and roadblocks that Islam puts in the way of those who leave it. Another is direct persecution.

Yet another reason can be disappointment with Christians and with church. When people who are trying to leave Islam approach nearby Christians seeking guidance and help, they can experience rejection and unexpected barriers to full acceptance within the Christian community. Many have even been turned away by churches. This is due to fear, which is caused by Islam's demand that *dhimmis* must not help anyone to leave Islam. Helping someone leave Islam puts the Christian community at risk because it removes the 'protection' provided to non-Muslims.

To be able to change this pattern of rejection of converts by Christians, the church needs to understand and reject the *dhimma* covenant and the burdens it imposes. As long as churches and individual Christians remain spiritually bound by the influence of the *dhimma*, they will experience deep spiritual pressure not to help those who leave Islam. To solve this problem the church needs to resist, renounce, and reject the *dhimma* system.

Another reason for people falling away is that the influence of Islam on their soul continues on, shaping the way they think and relate to others. This can make it easier to return to Islam than to continue as a Christian. It is like getting new shoes: sometimes the old shoes just seem to fit more easily and feel more comfortable.

Unfruitful discipleship

A second problem can be unfruitful discipleship. People with a Muslim background can experience strong emotional and spiritual blockages and controls which prevent spiritual growth. Common issues include fear, a sense of insecurity and love of money, feelings of rejection, a sense of victimhood, taking offense, inability to trust others, emotional pain, sexual sin, gossip, and lying. All of these can stop people from growing.

An underlying cause for such problems is the ongoing controlling influence of Islam. For example, in Islam there is an emphasis on being superior to others, and Muslims are thought to be superior to non-Muslims. In a culture of superiority, people gain comfort from feeling better than others. In a church this can cause competitiveness. For example, if one person is appointed as a leader, others are offended because they weren't appointed. The need to feel superior also stirs up a culture of gossip, which provides a way to pull other people down. People may gossip because they can think themselves to be better than those being gossiped about. Another problem can be a spirit of offense, which is empowered by the way Muhammad responded to rejection.

There was a young man from Iraq who became a Christian and gained asylum in Canada. He tried attending churches, but every time he attended a new church he would take offense at something, and would criticize the other churchgoers as hypocrites. This man ended up living a very isolated, lonely life, still a Christian but completely cut off from any Christian community. This meant that his growth in discipleship was completely halted: he was unable to grow into maturity. He could not be fruitful.

Unhealthy churches

One of the great challenges facing new believers is finding a healthy church. The church is not a resort for the righteous, but a hospital for sinners—or that is what it should be. Sinners do belong in church, but just as people can get sick in a hospital, when the members of a church are not growing in Christian maturity, their sins and problems can be amplified and cause damage to the whole community. This can tear churches apart and cause them to fail. Just as unhealthy Christians can create unhealthy churches, unhealthy churches can in their turn make it hard for their members to grow into healthy maturity.

If church members are gossiping about their pastor, eventually they will have a damaged pastor, or no pastor at all. Everyone will suffer. This will also cause divisions and breakdown in the church community, and few people will want to serve as a leader in such a church. As another example, if church members tend to think in a competitive way, desiring to be superior to others, this can cause churches in the same city to be critical of each other, each claiming that it is the better church. Instead of these churches experiencing the great blessing of working together, they see each other as threats rather than partners in the gospel.

The need to stay free

Recall from Lesson 2 that Satan is an accuser, and his key strategy is to accuse Christian believers. To accuse them he will exploit any 'legal rights' he has against them, such as unconfessed sin, unforgiveness, words that bind us (including oaths, vows, and covenants), wounds of the soul, and generational curses. To become free, disciples of Christ need to cancel these 'legal rights', get rid of footholds, and shut open doors.

In Matthew 12:43-45, Jesus tells a parable of how, when an evil spirit has been expelled from a person, it can come back to occupy the person again, bringing seven other spirits worse than itself, so the person's situation at the end will be much worse than before the demon was first cast out. The image Jesus uses in the parable is of a house, swept clean and empty, ready to be occupied again. How do the spirits re-occupy this house? First, a door must have been left open; and second, the house is "unoccupied" (Matthew 12:44).

So here are two problems:

1. A door has been left open.

2. The house was left empty.

To build a healthy church, we need healthy Christians. And to be healthy a Christian needs to be free. This means the person must close all the open doors that Satan might exploit, and their soul must be filled with good things to replace the evil that has been cast out.

All the doors need to be closed. Every single one! Something important about spiritual freedom is that it is not enough to just close one open door. They all need to be closed. It is no good to have the best lock in the world on the back door of a house if the front door is left wide open. If we deny one legal right that Satan has been using against a person, but don't deal with the others, the person is not yet free.

To get free is one thing. To stay free is another. Equally important as closing doors is filling the house and not leaving it empty. This includes praying for a person to be filled with the Holy Spirit. It also means cultivating a godly way of living, so one's soul is filled up with good things.

Suppose a person's bondage is due to lies they have believed and spoken. The lies need to be renounced, and, in addition, the person needs to embrace, meditate on, and take delight in the truth. Out with the lies, in with the truth!

Consider a different situation: a person who has been afflicted by a demon of hatred, which has led to bad actions, including many hateful curses spoken against other people. When this demon of hatred is cast out, the person needs not only to renounce and reject hatred, but also to cultivate a lifestyle of loving and blessing others, building their own soul up instead of tearing it down. They need to change their habits and their whole way of thinking. The church community plays an essential role in helping a person stay free. They can help a person renew and rebuild their soul, to become a transformed person.

Paul often writes about this process in his letters. He is constantly praying and working for the believers to be built up in truth and love. He is always remembering what the believers once were and sometimes he reminds people of this, to give encouragement to keep growing:

> At one time we too were foolish, disobedient, deceived and enslaved by all kinds of passions and pleasures. We lived in malice and envy, being hated and hating one another. (Titus 3:3)

But disciples of Christ should not live like this anymore. We have been changed, and are meant to go on being changed to become more and more like Jesus, who was blameless, with no legal rights given to Satan. So Paul writes to the Philippians:

> … this is my prayer: that your love may abound more and more in knowledge and depth of insight, so that you may be able to discern what is best and may be pure and blameless for the day of Christ, filled with the fruit of righteousness that comes through Jesus Christ—to the glory and praise of God. (Philippians 1:9-11)

What a beautiful picture of a healthy disciple, growing in love, in knowledge, and in wisdom; pure and blameless; and bearing good fruit which brings praise to God! This person has not only been set free, but the house of their soul, instead of being dangerously "unoccupied," is being filled with the good things of Jesus Christ.

A key role of the church, and of the pastor, is to help disciples live like this: to close all the open doors to Satan and help believers to be filled up with all the good things of Christ.

Forming disciples is a great calling and there is much to learn about it. Here we will consider how to support healthy growth in disciples who have been set free from the bondages of Islam.

Healing and deliverance

We have emphasized the need to close all the doors and remove all the footholds. In any one disciple's life some of these could be due directly to the influence of Islam, and the prayer resources provided here can be used to close the door on Islam.

However, disciples of Christ can have other bondages in their lives not due directly to Islam. These can be due to any of the areas described in Lesson 2: unconfessed sin, unforgiveness, soul wounds, words and associated ritual acts, lies, and generational curses. In the lives of former Muslims one can observe the damaging effects of:

- unforgiveness
- abusive fathers
- family breakdown (divorce, polygamy)
- drug addiction
- the occult and witchcraft
- sexual trauma (due to assault, rape, incest)
- violence
- generational curses
- anger
- rejection and self-rejection
- women distrusting and hating men

- men having contempt for women.

Many of these areas can be influenced by the impact of Islam on culture and family life, but people also have their own personal spiritual baggage, accumulated during their lives. In order to progress to Christian maturity we need to be set free from these things, not just from Islam.

One young man suffered from a family condition that caused severe stomach problems: most of his relatives had died of stomach cancer. The doctors in Iran and Australia had told him he had a pre-cancerous condition in his stomach for which he had to take constant medication. At one point he discerned that this could be caused by a curse on his family. He renounced and broke this generational curse and dedicated himself anew to God. He was completely healed and stopped taking all medications. What was also remarkable was that at the same time he was healed of a tendency to get easily stressed and suffer from anxiety. He became much calmer and more trusting of God in his life circumstances. This healing and deliverance was an essential step in preparing him to bear the stresses of serving as a pastor.

To have a healthy church, ministry that deals with all kinds of open doors and footholds needs to be a normal part of the pastoral care of believers. Remember, when securing a house, it is not enough to close just one door or the door of the covenants of Islam: *all* the openings to the house must be closed.

Teaching into the gaps

Imagine an old, ruined house. The roof is leaky; you can even see the sky through it. The windows, which were once glass, are broken and the wind blows freely through them. The doors are torn off their hinges, lying outside on the ground. Inside, walls are broken, with holes punched in them. The floor is rotten. The foundations are cracked and broken. And there are squatters in the house who do not own it. They should not be there and they are actually destroying the house.

A lot of work is needed to restore this house. The first step is to make the house secure: to fix the roof and put in new windows and solid doors with locks, so no more squatters can get in. This is the first step in this ministry of freedom: close all the open doors. It needs to be done first because if all the doors are not closed, the squatters (the demons) can just come back through one of the open doors.

Once the house is secure, other work can start: restoring the foundations, repairing the walls, and making the house beautiful and comfortable to live in.

When former Muslims come to Christ, they can bring damage to the soul with them, caused by Islam and Islamic culture, which needs to be restored.

A believer's soul is like a bucket. We are intended to hold pure, sweet water: the water of life which comes from Jesus Christ. This is what our life is meant to be like. But if the bucket has a hole or gap in its side—like a weakness in our character—then the bucket cannot hold as much water. The bucket can only hold water up to the lowest hole or gap in its side. In order for this bucket to hold more water, we need to fill in that gap.

All over the world, this soul damage has a similar pattern wherever Islam has taken root. As Don Little has pointed out, "the influence of Islam in diverse settings creates similar obstacles for BMBs seeking to live for Christ."[17]

Another way to think about this is to consider what happens when someone has a bad accident, and they take a long time to recover. Normally some of their muscles will grow weak and even waste away because of lack of use. In order to fully recover, such a person can be helped by very specific exercises to strengthen the weak muscles (physiotherapy). These exercises can take a long time and be quite painful, but they are essential to enable the whole body to work again as it should. You can only get as much done as your weakest muscle allows you to.

What this means is that the teaching program for a church of Believers from Muslim Backgrounds needs to carefully and systematically address this damage. We call this 'teaching into the gaps': speaking biblical truth into areas where lies formerly ruled. There are many different areas that need to be addressed.

---

17. Don Little, *Effective Discipling in Muslim Communities*, p. 170.

One of the emphases of Muhammad was the superiority of one person over another; for example, of Muslims over non-Muslims. He considered it shameful to be inferior or below another person. In Islamic societies it is usually part of the cultural emotional worldview to want to be better than other people. One Christian declared that in Iranian culture, people are happy when they see another person fall over in the street, or they hear that someone has failed an exam. They are happy because they were not the one who fell or failed, so they feel superior.

This way of viewing a person's worth can cause many problems in churches. For example, people at one church may claim that their church is superior to other churches. This attitude causes offense, so that the churches in an area refuse to work together. With this attitude, if one person is appointed to a leadership role, another person may feel rejected, and be jealous, asking, "Why didn't they choose me? Do they think I am no good?" This problem can be so bad that people refuse to make themselves available for leadership roles because they fear they will be attacked and criticized by other people in the church.

With this attitude, people often do not know how to humbly offer constructive feedback to make improvements in the life of the church. Instead they speak as if they were the experts, talking with pride, and correcting other people in an insensitive way.

Such an attitude also incites gossip, as people gain pleasure from tearing others down.

To address this deep problem it is essential to teach about cultivating a servant's heart: people need to learn why Jesus washed his disciple's feet, and hear his command to do the same. People also need to be taught to find their identity in Christ, and not in what they do or what other people say or think about them. They need to be taught to "boast" about and "delight" in their weaknesses (2 Corinthians 12:9-10). They need to learn that loving others means rejoicing in other people's successes and grieving when they are suffering or in sorrow (Romans 12:15; 1 Corinthians 12:26). People also need teaching about how to speak the truth in love. Believers also need to be taught about the destructive effects of gossip, and how to respond well if there is a complaint about a brother or sister.

Another problem for people coming from Islam to Christ can be learning to speak the truth. In Islamic cultures, people can be trained not to be transparent and open (see Lesson 7 on deception), often to avoid shame. For example, suppose you see a fellow Christian at church and sense they are struggling with something, so you ask "How are you? Are you okay?" In fact, there is a problem, and the person is not okay, but they say, "I'm fine thanks. Everything is good." In this way, they keep their mask on. Such a tendency to hide one's problems is common among people who have left Islam. Satan uses this to stop disciples from growing, by preventing them from asking for help.

To address this issue, disciples need repeated teaching about the importance of speaking the truth to each other, and why this is so important for personal growth and freedom.

There are many other areas of Islamic cultures where 'teaching into the gaps' is needed, such as:

- the need for forgiveness and knowing how to apply it
- overcoming a tendency to easily feel rejected and take offense at others
- learning to minister in a way that builds trust between people
- renouncing witchcraft practices
- women and men learning to respect each other, and learning to speak the truth in their relationship, in a loving, humble way, without pride
- parents learning to bless their children instead of cursing them.

(See the list of issues caused by Islam and following Muhammad's example at the end of Lesson 4.)

It is very important to emphasize that 'teaching into the gaps' needs to be systematic and thorough, going deeply into issues so people can rebuild their whole emotional and theological worldview.

In these sections we consider how to form believers and leaders.

Start well

Don Little contrasts two missionaries working among Muslims in North Africa. Both had worked there for years.[18]

Steve could quickly lead Muslims to make a commitment to Christ, sometimes within his first conversation with them. However, almost every one of these converts would fall away, often within a few weeks of deciding to follow Jesus. Few lasted more than a year. Steve's technique was to lead people to faith in Christ quickly, and to trust the Holy Spirit to help them grow and learn more about the Christian faith.

Cheri's approach and success rate was the opposite. She would take a long time before leading people to Christ, sometimes years. She only invited the women she was working with to become disciples when she was sure they understood fully what conversion to Christ would mean, including the possibility of persecution and divorce by their husbands. Every single woman she led to Christ became a strongly committed believer, whose faith continued even after Cheri was expelled from North Africa.

It is essential when leading Muslims to Christ and discipling them that their process of initiation is thorough. Recall the six steps of following Christ from Lesson 5:

1. Two confessions:

   ▪ I am a sinner and cannot save myself.

   ▪ There is only one God, the creator, who sent his Son Jesus to die for my sins.

2. Turning away (repenting) from my sins and from all that is evil.

3. Requests for forgiveness, freedom, eternal life, and the Holy Spirit.

4. Transfer of allegiance to Christ as Lord of my life.

---

18. Don Little, *Effective Discipling in Muslim Communities*, pp. 26-27.

5. Promise and consecration of my life to submit to and serve Christ.

6. Declaration of my identity in Christ.

It seems that Steve was taking new converts through steps 1-2, and perhaps step 3, but not securing them in steps 4-6. A full transfer of allegiance (step 4) requires cutting ties with Islam and replacing these with total allegiance to Jesus. The promise and consecration (step 5) must include coming to terms with persecution and this also requires an understanding of biblical ethics: to consecrate yourself you need to understand what kind of life you are consecrated to live. The declaration of a new identity (step 6) requires an understanding of Christian identity and what it means to be a child of God through Jesus Christ instead of just a "submitter" to Allah. This also means understanding what it means to lose your old identity through being excluded from the *Umma*, including potential separation from friends and family.

In addition, step 3 requires a mature understanding of what it means to be free in Christ, what it means to forgive others, and the nature of life in the Spirit.

To really commit deeply to these steps with full understanding a process of discipleship is required. Through this process someone can learn to carefully and thoughtfully set aside the Islamic outlook and replace it with a biblical one.

When someone turns to Christ and commits to follow him, they are in effect declaring war on Satan. They are committing themselves to plunder Satan's rights, and hand all rights over their life to Jesus Christ. This is not a simple or superficial decision. It has to be backed by the fully engaged understanding and will of the person.

For these reasons, ministers of the gospel are advised to be slow to baptize, and slow to lead people in a prayer of commitment to follow Jesus. They should only do that when the person fully understands what it means for them and the people they love.

It is also recommended not to baptize anyone until they have prayed the 'Declaration and Prayer to Renounce the *Shahada* and Break Its Power' (see Lesson 5), with full understanding and commitment. This act should be preceded by teaching to explain its significance. This should be done some time before baptism. A renunciation prayer can also be included as part of the baptism ritual. This renunciation allows a full commitment to step 4: a full transfer of allegiance to Jesus Christ as Lord, which means rejecting all claims of Islam on one's life.

Mentor emerging leaders

One of the greatest needs facing Believers from a Muslim Background in the world today is more mature pastors who are also BMBs. Unhealthy leaders grow unhealthy churches. In order to have a healthy church, where people grow in maturity and freedom, a church needs healthy leaders. It is so very important to invest in BMB leaders who can lead healthy churches. This investment requires years of care and support.

Before you invest in potential leaders, you need to find them! A key principle is: be slow to advance people into leadership. If you advance someone too quickly you might regret this if someone better turns up later. People from an Islamic background can struggle with rejection and competitiveness, so before you raise someone up as a leader, make sure that:

- they are ready to be called

- they have the humility to take on a leadership role

- they are teachable

- they have the resilience to deal with the inevitable criticism they will receive.

If you are someone from a Muslim background who feels called to lead a church, do not seek the quickest or easiest way to prepare. Humbly understand that it will take time for you to be prepared. Be willing to submit to training. Be patient. Be teachable.

BMB leaders can be spoiled by being advanced too quickly. If they advance too quickly, they might not learn humility: they might think they know everything they need to know and they don't need more formation and training. With potential leaders it can be wise to make a series of short-term appointments initially, on a trial or trainee basis, and only gradually confirm them into a more permanent leadership role as they prove their calling and suitability in the eyes of the congregation. If people are advanced too quickly, before they have had the opportunity to prove themselves in the eyes of the congregation, they may experience early rejection before they are ready to cope with it, and this could damage their formation.

To nurture healthy leaders is very time-consuming and to develop mature Christian leaders a long-term perspective is essential. For any new believer who is a potential leader, growing into Christian maturity takes years. There is so much to learn, because for people coming from an Islamic background, certain ways of thinking and feeling about life and relationships have to be completely rebuilt.

Here are 12 key elements of mentoring leaders to maturity:

1. The person being trained (the trainee) should meet regularly with someone who is training them (the mentor), at least once a week.

2. Teach and show trainee leaders how to do theological reflection, integrating life experiences with faith. This is about learning to apply biblical and faith resources to the practical challenges of daily life and ministry. Through intentional theological reflection, a person's character is exposed to the truth, and can be gradually reshaped to conform more and more to the model of Jesus Christ.

3. Provide training in transparency and honesty: have high expectations for this. If a person being mentored is wearing a mask, only the mask will become mature! One day the real person might just walk out of the room and leave the mask behind. Then you will discover they were not the person you thought they were.

    It is also important for the mentor to model what it means to be transparent if he or she expects the potential leader to be open about their struggles.

    When I first began discipling a couple who were potential pastors for a church of former Muslims, at our first meeting I asked, "Do you have any problems?"

    They said, "No."

The next week we met again, so I asked again, "Do you have any problems?"

The answer came back: "No."

We met for the third week and I asked one more time, "Do you have any problems?"

Again the answer was "No."

Then I said, "I am very sorry to hear that. Either you have problems and you don't know it, which is not good, or you have problems and you are not telling me, which is also not good. Which one is it?"

Then the couple began to open up: they were experiencing problems, but their Islamic cultural background had taught them it was shameful to reveal weaknesses or difficulties to others. However, from that day forward our relationship was transformed as they shared openly about the difficulties and challenges they were facing. From then on I was able to help them. Through this process, trust was built, and they grew rapidly in Christian maturity.

4. Both the mentor and the potential leader need to be proactive and intentional in raising issues to work on. Encourage the trainee to be intentional about discerning issues and bringing them to your meetings.

5. The trainee and their mentor need to wrestle together with key problems and decisions affecting the life of the congregation. In this way the trainee leader can learn how to deal with challenging issues in pastoral ministry in a godly, biblical way.

6. As you mentor the trainee, help them walk in freedom. Almost everyone needs to be set free from something as part of their training for ministry. If bondages are not addressed and wounds healed, a lack of healing and freedom will limit a person's fruitfulness in the future. When issues come up that point to a lack of personal freedom, address the issue by applying the resources we have in Christ. These are described in Lesson 2. Also, someone who has been through the process of being set free will understand better how to help others be free.

7. Train the BMB trainee in self-care. It is important for BMB leaders to learn to care for themselves, and for their families, as a high priority. There are many challenges in this difficult ministry, and if a pastor does not make it a priority to care first for their own self, and for their family, they might not last long. If a pastor is not caring for their own family, their ministry might not be trusted. People will ask, "How can they care for the church if they cannot care for their own family?"

8. If your leaders are a couple, they will need support to grow in understanding of what it means to have a Christian marriage based on servant-hearted mutual love and respect, not on dominance and control of one person by the other.

9. Emphasize the importance of self-awareness in ministry. When people are competitive, lack transparency, and want to feel superior to others, they will lack self-awareness. This can be part of the damage caused by Islam. In order to grow, a person being mentored has to learn to value critical feedback as a precious gift and resource. This means learning not to be defensive or feel threatened, offended or rejected when feedback is critical. At the same time, a mentor must model a receptive and open approach, modeling self-awareness in how they seek and respond to feedback. If trainees can see that the mentor is able to receive critical feedback, they will be better able to receive it themselves.

10. Help the trainee to process disappointments in a godly way so they can become resilient. Equip the trainee BMB leader in how to apply biblical faith resources when they are let down by others, or life's circumstances seem overwhelming.

11. Equip for spiritual warfare. Ministering to people coming to Christ always involves pushback from the evil one: they cannot avoid it. Believers from a Muslim Background need to be trained to hold their ground during times when Satan is attacking.

12. Model trust and cooperation with other Christians, and cultivate godly partnerships with other ministries. This is essential for BMBs to grow in discerning the body of Christ: it

honors God and is a way to receive God's blessing for your church. This is also a good way to teach humility.

Study Guide

Lesson 8

Bible in this lesson

2 Timothy 2:20-21
Matthew 12:43-45
Titus 3:3
Philippians 1:9-11

2 Corinthians 12:9-10
Romans 12:15
1 Corinthians 12:26

There are no quranic references, no new vocabulary and no new names in this lesson.

Questions Lesson 8

- Discuss the case study.

Falling away

1. What four reasons does Durie give for some people returning to Islam after deciding to follow Jesus?

2. Why do churches sometimes turn Muslims away when they are asking to learn more about Jesus and Christianity?

3. What should churches do in order to be able to support Muslims turning to Christ?

Unfruitful discipleship

4. What does Durie say are common issues faced by former Muslims who become Christians?

5. What is the underlying cause of many of these problems?

6. How can appointing a leader cause problems in a church?

7. Why did the asylum seeker who went to Canada cut himself off from other Christians?

Unhealthy churches

8. How can the desire to feel superior stop churches from working together?

The need to stay free

9. What two problems are illustrated by Jesus' parable of the empty house?

10. What do you need to build a healthy church?

11. What needs to change after someone is set free?

12. Why does Paul remind Titus of what they both once used to be like?

13. How did Paul's earlier life fit his description of life before following Jesus?

14. How can a believer fill the 'house' of their soul, and not leave it unoccupied, according to what Paul writes in Philippians 1:9-11?

Healing and deliverance

15. Durie reports 12 negative effects in the lives of converts. How many of these have you observed?

16. What did the young man do to be healed of a pre-cancerous stomach condition? What was the other change he experienced after he was healed?

17. What is important to do in order to make a house properly secure?

Teaching into the gaps

18. What is the first step in the ministry of freedom and why is it the first step?

19. How is the human soul like a bucket of water?

20. What similarities has Don Little observed in BMBs all over the world?

21. Why might some people feel happy to hear about other people's troubles?

22. What are some of the problems for churches when believers want to be superior to others in the church?

23. What six teachings does Durie suggest can help correct the problem of people wanting to feel superior to others?

24. What does Durie say can be a problem caused by not speaking the truth?

25. What six areas of Islamic culture does Durie identify which need "teaching into the gaps"?

26. Why should 'teaching into the gaps' be systematic and thorough?

Start well

27. What were the differences between the approaches of Steve and Cheri, and why was Cheri's approach more successful?

28. Can you list the six steps of the 'Declaration and Prayer of Commitment to Follow Jesus' from memory? If not, memorize them as a group by repeating them until everyone can name them in order.

29. In the light of the six steps, what steps did Steve seem to be missing when he led people to Christ?

30. Who are you declaring war on when you turn to Christ?

31. What should be done before someone who has left Islam is ready to be baptized?

Mentor emerging leaders

32. What does Durie believe is a great need facing Muslim Background Believers in the world today? Do you agree?

33. Why does Durie say that it is better to advance leaders slowly?

34. What can happen if leaders are advanced too quickly?

35. When mentoring a trainee leader how often should you meet with them, according to Durie?

36. What is theological reflection and how does it help people grow in maturity?

37. Why is it important for a mentor to be open and transparent with the person they are training?

38. In the story Durie told, why was the trainee reluctant to seek help for the problems he was facing?

39. Why should a mentor involve the trainee in making decisions about important problems in the life of the congregation?

40. Why is it important to be able to minister freedom to a person in training to be a leader?

41. Why is self-care important in ministry?

42. What should a Christian marriage be based upon?

43. Why is self-awareness so important and how can the influence of Islam prevent this?

44. Why is it important for a mentor to be open to receiving criticism?

45. Why should a pastor of a BMB congregation be trained for spiritual warfare?

46. Why is it important that leaders of BMB churches learn to respect and work well with other churches?

Additional Resources

For more information about many of the topics about Islam taught here, please consult *The Third Choice: Islam, Dhimmitude and Freedom* by Mark Durie.

Liberty to the Captives resources in many different languages, including the prayers, can be found on the site luke4-18.com.

For more information about the steps needed to set people free from demons, Mark Durie recommends the book *Free in Christ* by Pablo Bottari. It is available in English and Spanish. He also recommends the training resources at freemin.org (in English and some other languages).

Here are some additional prayers to help set people free.

Forgiveness Prayer[19]

Father, you have made it clear that you require me to forgive. You desire the healing and freedom for me that forgiveness brings.

Today, I choose to forgive all who have set me up to enter into sin [name them], *and all who have hurt me* [name them]. *I choose to release them, each and every one, for* [name the wrongs they have done].

I let go of all judgments against them, and I let go of all punishments for them which I have harbored in my heart. I turn [name them] *over to you, for you are the only righteous judge.*

Lord, please forgive me for allowing my own reactions to hurt others and to hurt myself.

---

19. This and the next two prayers are based on prayers in *Restoring the Foundations* by Chester and Betsy Kylstra.

On the basis of your forgiveness I choose to forgive myself for allowing this hurt to affect my attitudes and behavior.

Holy Spirit, I thank you for working forgiveness into my life, for giving me the grace I need to forgive, and for continuing to enable me to forgive.

In Jesus' name,

Amen.

A Prayer to Renounces Lies (Ungodly Beliefs)

Father, I confess my sin (and my ancestors' sin) of believing the lie that [name the lie].

I forgive those who contributed to forming this ungodly belief, especially [name them].

I repent of this sin, and ask you Lord to forgive me for receiving this ungodly belief, for living my life based on it, and for any way in which I have judged others because of it. I receive your forgiveness now [wait and receive from God].

On the basis of your forgiveness, Lord, I choose to forgive myself for believing the lie.

I renounce and break all agreements I have made with this ungodly belief. I cancel my agreements with the kingdom of darkness. I break all associated agreements I have made with demons.

Lord, what truth do you want to reveal to me about this ungodly belief? [Wait and listen to the Lord, so you can then declare the truth that corrects the lie.]

I declare the truth that [name the truth].

In Jesus' name,

Amen.

A Prayer for Generational Sin

I confess the sins of my ancestors, my parents' sins, and my own sins of [name sin(s)].

I choose to forgive and release my ancestors, as well as all others who have influenced me, for these sins and resulting curses, and for the consequences in my life [name them specifically].

I ask you to forgive me, Lord, for these sins: for yielding to them and to the curses. I receive your forgiveness.

On the basis of your forgiveness, Lord, I choose to forgive myself for entering into these sins.

I renounce the sin and curses of [name them].

I break the power of these sins and curses from my life and from the lives of my descendants through the redemptive work of Christ on the cross.

I receive your freedom from these sins and the resulting curses. I receive [specifically name God's blessings that you are, in faith, receiving].

In Jesus' name,

Amen.

Answers

Lesson I answers

1. The Spirit told him to renounce Islam.

2. One of the most urgent needs is to renounce Islam.

3. The *shahada* and the *dhimma*.

4. A Muslim who has chosen to follow Christ.

5. A non-Muslim.

6. The surrender of the convert to the religion of Islam and the surrender of non-Muslims under Islamic dominance.

7. The confession of the strict oneness of Allah and the prophethood of Muhammad.

8. The law of Islam that determines the dominated status of Christians.

9. That Christians who have never been Muslims need to renounce the claims of the *dhimma*.

10. That *sharia* law should be supreme and rule over all other principles of justice or power.

11. All spiritual claims upon their soul except Christ's.

12. Out of spiritual darkness and into Christ's rule.

13. Political and community action, human rights advocacy, academic inquiry, use of the media, and at times a military response from national governments.

14. Conversion, political surrender or the sword.

15. More than a thousand years; almost 800 years.

16. He promised them assurance of paradise if they gave their life in defending Christendom.

17. Islam's root power is spiritual.

18. To the fierce king and master of intrigue of Daniel's prophecy.

19. Islam's:

- sense of … superiority
- hunger for … success
- use of … deception
- co-opting the strength and riches … of others
- defeating nations … who have a false sense of security
- opposition … to the Son of God
- track-record of … devastating Christians and Jews.

20. Not by human power.

21. The power of Christ and his cross.

Lesson 2 answers

1. He found he couldn't say the word Muhammad.

2. He was set free from anger and became effective in evangelism and discipling others.

3. The birthright of every Christian is the glorious freedom of the children of God.

4. In Nazareth.

5. The promise of freedom.

6. Freedom from hopelessness, hunger, sickness, demons.

7. The prisoner must walk out through the unlocked door. Spiritual freedom is something we need to choose.

8. Thief. Prince of this world. God of this age. Ruler of the kingdom of the air. They teach us that Satan has power in this world.

9. Satan has genuine but limited power and sovereignty.

10. The worldview of Islam and its spiritual power.

11. In bondage to demonic powers.

12. Satan's power and the power of darkness.

13. We are brought into the kingdom of Jesus Christ, and we are forgiven and set free.

14. That they have been transferred into the kingdom of Jesus Christ.

15. Five aspects: 1) Renounce Satan and all evil. 2) Renounce all ungodly ties to other people. 3) Renounce all ungodly covenants. 4) Renounce ungodly abilities. 5) Hand over our life to Jesus Christ as Lord.

16. Conflict between God and Satan; between two kingdoms.

17. The church can be a battleground, and it can be exploited for evil.

18. Christians can be certain of victory through the cross.

19. The comparison with the Roman triumph shows that the demons have lost their power and they have been humiliated.

20. Accuser or adversary.

21. Christians are warned to be alert.

22. Our sins and parts of our lives that have been surrendered to Satan.

23. Sin, unforgiveness, words (and symbolic actions), soul wounds, ungodly beliefs (lies), and generational sin and resulting curses.

24. To be able to name and reject claims Satan might make against us.

25. An open door is an entry point granted to Satan. A foothold is ground within the soul that Satan claims has been given over to him.

26. Legal rights; spiritual ground that may be occupied by Satan.

27. It means Satan has no opportunity to make a claim against us.

28. Satan could find no sin he could use to make a claim against Jesus.

29. Jesus' innocence is important because it means Satan could not claim the crucifixion was a just punishment.

30. We need to shut open doors and remove footholds.

31. By repenting of our sins.

32. We must forgive others first.

33. He can use our unforgiveness to claim a foothold against us.

34. Forgiving others; receiving God's forgiveness; forgiving ourselves.

35. No: forgiveness is different from forgetting.

36. Satan can use the hurt to feed lies to us.

37. She found healing from traumatic experiences of abuse by her house 'guests'. She had to renounce intimidation.

38. Pour out your soul to the Lord; pray for healing; forgive the person who caused the wound; renounce fear (or other harmful effects); confess and reject any lies.

39. For every word we have spoken.

40. Because this can give him an opportunity to use our words against us.

41. The blood of Jesus.

42. May I become like this animal: may the same thing happen to me if I break the covenant.

43. They invoke a curse of death upon the person who agrees to the covenant.

44. Decapitation.

45. Satan feeds lies to us.

46. Identify and reject lies that previously we had accepted as true.

47. "Real men don't cry."

48. The lie that feels true.

49. A truth encounter can enable us to confess, reject, and renounce the lies we used to believe.

50. A bad spiritual inheritance.

51. Parental influence and bad examples.

52. A system of blessings and curses.

53. Adam and Eve unleashed intergenerational curses: pain, dominance, decay, and death.

54. This is a promise for the Messianic Age: for the kingdom of Jesus Christ.

55. Confess our ancestors' sins and our own sins; reject and renounce these sins; break all associated curses.

56. Authority over Satan.

57. Because it says that everything must be completely destroyed together with the idols.

58. The cross has the power to break evil pacts we have entered into.

59. Actions that are specific.

60. "I will never love anyone else again." Susan became bitter and hostile. She renounced that vow.

61. Five steps: 1. Confess and repent. 2. Renounce. 3. Break. 4. Cast out. 5. Bless and fill.

62. Confess sin and declare the truth.

63. Bless them with the opposite of what afflicted them.

Lesson 3 answers

1. Submission to Allah as sovereign master.

2. A Muslim.

3. Muhammad, the final messenger of Allah.

4. The Quran contains Muhammad's revelations, and the *Sunna* contain his teachings and actions.

5. The example of Muhammad is recorded in the *hadiths* (traditional sayings) and in the *siras* (the biographies of Muhammad).

6. Muhammad.

7. All that Muhammad did becomes the standard.

8. Those who obey Allah and his messenger.

9. Hellfire.

10. Anyone who rejects Muhammad's message.

11. Murder, torture, rape, abuse of women, enslavement, theft, deception, and incitement against non-Muslims.

12. You must believe in and obey the Quran.

13. The *Sunna* is like the body and the Quran is like the backbone.

14. Muslims rely on an expert minority.

15. There can be no Islam without *sharia* laws.

16. The *sharia* is thought to be divinely mandated.

17. It is the call to success.

18. People are divided into winners and the rest—the losers.

19. Muslims are taught that they are superior to non-Muslims; pious Muslims are superior to less devout Muslims.

20. Genuine Muslims, hypocrites, idolaters, and People of the Book.

21. A *mushrik* 'associator'.

22. Four things condemned: 1) Their scriptures are corrupted. 2) They follow a distorted version of Islam. 3) They have gone astray. 4) They are ignorant and in need of being liberated by Muhammad.

23. On the positive side, the Quran says Christians and Jews are faithful and truly believe.

24. Four claims: 1) Christians are to live under their superiority. 2) Muslims are destined to rule over us. 3) We are to be fought against. 4) We are denounced as going to hell.

25. Jews will have greater enmity against Muslims than Christians.

26. It is the best-known chapter in the Quran, and it is mandatory to repeat it daily. It is said up to 17 times a day or 5,000 times a year.

27. Christians (gone astray) and Jews (earned Allah's anger).

28. The life and teaching of Muhammad.

29. Islamization.

30. Six problems: 1) Women have inferior status. 2) The teaching of *jihad*. 3) Cruel and excessive punishments. 4) *Sharia* cannot make people good. 5) Encouragement of lying. 6) Persecution of non-Muslims, including Christians.

31. *Sharia* courts were introduced in Nigeria.

32. The judge followed Muhammad's example.

33. 1) It is excessive. 2) It is cruel. 3) It damages men who do the stoning. 4) It targets women. 5) It makes an infant an orphan. 6) It ignores the possibility of rape.

34. They can lie when they are in danger from non-Muslims. Husbands may lie to their wives. They can lie when they are entrusted with a secret, in warfare, etc.

35. It is the practice of deception in order to keep Muslims safe.

36. It destroys truth and creates confusion.

37. The guidance of their religious experts.

38. Study Islam for yourself, even if Islam's leadership tries not to mention or discuss many things in public.

39. To follow Jesus or Muhammad.

40. Isa (Jesus).

41. The way of life (*sharia*) of previous prophets.

42. A book given to Isa (Jesus) by Allah.

43. Isa will destroy Christianity and force everyone to become Muslims.

44. Muslims are taught that if they follow Muhammad, they are following Jesus.

45. This teaching conceals God's saving plan and can prevent Muslims from following the true Jesus.

46. We can know about the real Jesus from the four Gospels.

47. Only through the Jesus of the Gospels can we find freedom from spiritual bondages.

Lesson 4 answers

1. Three pains: 1. Death of his father. 2. Death of his mother. 3. Humble task of being a shepherd boy for his uncle. (Also death of his grandfather.)

2. His contempt for Muhammad.

3. Six aspects: 1) She was his employer. 2) She was older. 3) She proposed to him. 4) She had been married twice already. 5) She was powerful and wealthy. 6) She got her father drunk in order to gain his approval to marry Muhammad.

4. Most of their children died, leaving Muhammad no male heir.

5. Muhammad's uncle Abu Talib and his wife Khadijah.

6. He was 40 and he was so troubled that he almost committed suicide.

7. Muhammad was a prophet not a madman.

8. Muhammad feared being rejected as a fraud.

9. Khadijah and Ali, Muhammad's younger cousin.

10. Muhammad mocked the Meccan gods.

11. He protected Muhammad from angry Meccans.

12. A total boycott, persecution of vulnerable Muslims, and abuse of Muhammad.

13. 83 Muslim men fled to Abyssinia (modern Ethiopia) with their families.

14. To worship both Allah and the Meccan gods.

15. That the prayers to three daughters of Allah—al-Lat, al-Uzza, and Manat—were approved.

16. All true prophets are occasionally led astray.

17. Boasts: 1) None of his ancestors was born out of wedlock. 2) He was the best man. 3) He was from the best clan (Hashim). 4) He was from the best tribe (Quraysh). 5) He was from the best nation (the Arabs).

18. Success in war.

19. Both Khadijah and his protector Abu Talib died. After Ta'if rejected him, Medinan Arabs pledged to protect him.

20. A group of *jinn* (demons) became Muslims.

21. The idea of *jinn* who converted to Islam, and teaching in the Quran and *hadiths* that every person has a familiar spirit, known as a *qarin*.

22. To wage war in complete obedience to the apostle.

23. He preached unhindered and most Medinan Arabs converted to Islam.

24. Torments in the afterlife for those who reject Islam.

25. Slaughter.

26. *Fitna.*

27. *Fitna* against Islam.

28. The existence of any obstacle to people entering Islam.

29. You deserve to be fought and killed.

30. Because the guilt of rejecting Islam is worse than death.

31. Millions of Muslims are dying but only dozens of non-Muslims.

32. He sought retribution and vindication, even from those who had died.

33. His hatred of being rejected.

34. They became permanently marked as guilty, deserving to be dominated as inferiors.

35. Aggressive responses to *fitna*.

36. Allah forbade him to obey it.

37. Slay them wherever you find them.

38. Some were believing, some not, but Islam would bless them.

39. He encouraged prayers and zakat alms like the Jews; he directed his prayers to al-Sham (Syria; i.e. Jerusalem); and he said his teaching was the same as theirs.

40. For self-validation against their increased criticisms.

41. He called the Jews deceivers, and he said they had falsified their scriptures.

42. Anti-Jewish messages:

    - Q4:46. Jews were cursed.

    - Q7:166, etc. Jews were monkeys and pigs.

    - Q5:70. Jews were prophet-killers.

    - Q5:13. Jews were hardened by Allah.

    - Q2:27. Jews were losers.

43. Judaism.

44. He threatened and then expelled them.

45. Because he was killing them and only conversion to Islam could protect them.

46. He accused them, attacked them, expelled them, and took their goods as booty.

47. He besieged them and then massacred the men, enslaving the women and children.

48. He invaded and conquered them but offered them the 'third choice': living as *dhimmis*.

49. Both Jews and Christians.

50. From self-rejection to self-validation to aggression.

51. The defeat and degradation of disbelievers.

52. An ideology and a military program.

53. Instead of being just a 'warner', he became a commander of believers, regulating their lives.

54. The way to obey Allah is to obey Muhammad.

55. They are based upon the evolution of Muhammad's own responses to being rejected.

56. Muhammad's problems have been passed on to the world through the *sharia*.

57. The words of the *shahada*.

58. That the Quran is Allah's word; and what the Quran says about Muhammad.

59. Reciting the *shahada* gives permission to spiritual authorities and powers to impose Muhammad's spiritual problems on Muslims.

60. [Participants will have circled negative aspects they have encountered.]

61. They deny it.

62. They say it is corrupted.

63. Destroy them.

64. The belief that the Quran is the word of God.

65. Instability, intimidation, vulnerability, and lack of confidence.

Lesson 5 answers

1. Rejection.

2. Four ways: 1) Shame of illegitimacy. 2) Very humble birth. 3) Herod's attempted murder of him. 4) Parents fled to Egypt like refugees.

3. The Pharisees attacked Christ with questions about the following:

   - Mark 3:2, etc. Breaking Sabbath laws.
   - Mark 11:28, etc. His authority.
   - Mark 10:2, etc. Divorce.
   - Mark 12:15, etc. Paying taxes to Caesar.
   - Matthew 22:36. The greatest commandment.
   - Matthew 22:42. The Messiah.
   - John 8:19. Jesus' paternity.
   - Matthew 22:23-28, etc. The resurrection.
   - Mark 8:11, etc. Miracles.

- Mark 3:22, etc. 'Having' Satan; doing miracles by Satan's power.

- Matthew 12:2, etc. His disciples' conduct.

- John 8:13. Giving invalid testimony.

4. Rejection that Jesus experienced:

  - Matt 2:16. Herod tried to kill him.

  - Mark 6:3, etc. Nazarenes tried to kill him.

  - Mark 3:21. Family insulted him.

  - John 6:66. Many followers deserted him.

  - John 10:31. Crowd tried to stone him.

  - John 11:50. Leaders plotted to kill him.

  - Mark 14:43-45, etc. Betrayed by Judas.

  - Mark 14:66-72, etc. Disowned by Peter.

  - Mark 15:12-15, etc. Crowd demanded death.

  - Mark 14:65, etc. Mocked by Jewish leader.

  - Mark 15:16-20, etc. Tortured by soldiers.

  - Mark 14:53-65., etc. Falsely condemned to death.

  - Deuteronomy 21:23. Cursed by crucifixion.

  - Mark 15:21-32, etc. Agonizing death with thieves.

5. Six responses: Jesus was not 1) aggressive or violent; 2) vengeful; 3) noisily quarrelsome. 4) He remained silent under accusation; and 5) he left places where they wanted to kill him.

6. He overcame the temptation and did not succumb to rejection.

7. Because he was very secure and at ease with himself.

8. Being rejected as the suffering servant of Isaiah.

9. His death by crucifixion.

10. The use of force to achieve his goals.

11. As symbolic, bringing divisions within families and possibly persecution.

12. He rejects the idea that the Messiah used violence, military force, or political options—that his kingdom was physical.

13. That they were prohibited from killing.

14. Christ taught the following about how to treat others:

    - Matthew 5:38-42, concerning evil: show good in return.

    - Matthew 7:1-5, concerning judging: do not judge others.

    - Matthew 5:43, concerning enemies: love them.

    - Matthew 5:5, concerning meekness: it will triumph.

    - Matthew 5:9, concerning peacemakers: they will be called children of God.

    - 1 Corinthians 4:11-13, etc., concerning persecution: Christians must endure great trials and not retaliate.

    - 1 Peter 2:21-25, concerning our example: Jesus is our example for loving others.

15. That they would experience flogging, hatred, betrayal and death.

16. To move on without bitterness.

17. When a Samaritan village refused to welcome him.

18. When violently persecuted: 1) Flee to another place. 2) Don't worry but rely on the Spirit. 3) Don't be afraid.

19. To rejoice when persecuted.

20. The hope of eternal life.

21. Three results: 1) People are alienated from God and from each other. 2) People are excluded from God's presence. 3) People are subjected to the curse of the Fall.

22. The incarnation and cross of Jesus Christ.

23. Jesus's submission to the cross.

24. He absorbed the hatred of his attackers and gave his life as a sacrifice for the sins of the world.

25. To the symbolic shedding of blood to atone for sin; and to the Isaiah 53 prophecy of the suffering servant.

26. Reconciliation with God.

27. Accusations from men, angels, or demons.

28. The ministry of reconciliation.

29. Vindicate himself by force.

30. Through his resurrection and ascension.

31. Vindication.

32. They regard suffering as a way of sharing in the sufferings of Christ.

33. Muhammad personally destroyed them and predicted that Isa will do the same when he returns to the earth.

34. The 'third choice' of dhimmitude, which allows non-Muslims to keep their faith.

35. He was forced to remove all religious symbols from his clothing.

Lesson 6 answers

1. Muhammad's "command to spread by the sword the faith he preached."

2. After conversion or war there is a third choice: surrender and live under Muslim's protection.

3. Convert to Islam; be killed; or surrender (and live in humiliation).

4. Fight until people testify that only Allah is to be worshipped, and Muhammad is the messenger of Allah (i.e. to the *shahada*).

5. Accept Islam, or demand *jizya*, or fight unbelievers.

6. Payment of tribute (*jizya*) and being disgraced, "made small."

7. The *dhimma* covenant.

8. *Dhimmis*.

9. Two principles: 1) Islam must triumph over other religions. 2) Muslims must be in a position of power to enforce Islam.

10. It is a head tax that acknowledges that they owe their heads to the conquering Muslims: the tax is a compensation for not being slain.

11. For the benefit of Muslims.

12. It is a compensation for being permitted to wear their heads that year.

13. The *jihad* starts again: war, looting, raping, and death.

14. The penalty for those who are defiant and become rebellious, which is *jihad*.

15. Freely available to be killed or captured.

16. Massacres due to accusations of having violated the *dhimma* covenant.

17. The sultan had appointed Jews to the position of Grand Vizier.

18. The Christians were accused of giving up their submissive status and with that, giving up their protection. Some converted to Islam to save their lives.

19. The ritual was enacted while paying the *jizya* tribute. It involved one or two blows on the neck and sometimes a ritual strangulation.

20. It is intended to express the *dhimmi* community's submissive acceptance of violent *jihad* if they break any of the conditions of their *dhimma*, up to and including decapitation of the men.

21. The curse of decapitation.

22. A blood pact or a blood oath, as in occult societies.

23. A self-cursing and permission for his own death penalty.

24. Gratitude and humble inferiority.

25. Examples:

   - Dhimmis' witness: not accepted in *sharia* courts.

   - Dhimmis' houses: not higher than Muslims' houses.

   - Dhimmis' horses: dhimmis not allowed to be mounted.

   - Dhimmis had to give way to Muslims on a road.

- Dhimmis' self-defense: not permitted.
- Dhimmis' religious symbols: not allowed in public.
- Dhimmis' churches: no repairs, and no new church buildings.
- Dhimmis' criticism of Islam: not allowed.
- Dhimmis' dress: not allowed to imitate Muslims.
- Dhimmis' marriages: a *dhimmi* man could not marry a Muslim woman, and if a Muslim man married a *dhimmi* woman, the children would be Muslims.

26. That they would pay *jizya* and be made "small."

27. As a killing of the soul.

28. The totality of conditions which a *dhimma* covenant produces.

29. To submissively get used to humiliation.

30. Feelings of inferiority, secretiveness, cunning, meanness, and fear.

31. As the religion of masters and rulers.

32. Their false sense of superiority and religious protectionism weakens Muslims and makes it hard for them to accept reality.

33. To slavery: slavery was abolished in the American Civil War, yet abusive racism continues more than a century later.

34. The claim that the West owes a debt to Islam for its civilization.

35. European nations.

36. The revival of the *sharia*.

37. Five consequences: 1) A wounded spirit. 2) A spirit of offense. 3) A victim mentality. 4) A spirit of violence. 5) A will to dominate others.

38. Muhammad's oppressed spiritual condition sought the degradation of others.

39. He refused to take offense, refused to resort to violence, refused to dominate others, and refused to adopt a wounded spirit.

40. None of the Christians had previously understood their spiritual bondage; all prayed to be freed; all were overjoyed when it was done.

41. Fear of jihadi attacks, past trauma from jihadists, past threats on your family.

42. They are designed first to cancel the *dhimma* covenant, breaking its claims over our lives, and second to reject and break all curses coming from dhimmitude.

43. They will help people be free of these influences.

Lesson 7 answers

1. The conviction to love truth and to speak the truth.

2. Because God is relational.

3. Lying.

4. He leads people astray.

5. Permitted forms of lying: in warfare, to a wife, to gain protection, to defend the *Umma*, and to gain protection when in danger (*taqiyya*).

6. To pretend to deny your own faith.

7. Their superiority and being better than non-Muslims.

8. Muhammad.

9. Concepts of honor and shame.

10. The emotional worldview of feeling superior.

11. Because there are conflicting statements in the *hadiths* about cursing.

12. Cursing non-Muslims.

13. Hatred, excitement, and a spiritual "charge."

14. A covenant that binds two people together.

15. Unforgiveness keeps a soul tie between two people.

16. [Students consider the prayer and identify for themselves the points where the steps apply.]

17. Renounced: the sin of cursing others, resulting curses, hatred of others, the emotion experienced, demons of hatred and cursing, all ungodly connections with Imams and others, all assignments of demons which maintain these soul ties. Broken: ungodly spiritual powers, curses, ungodly soul ties.

18. Freedom from curses, peace, gentleness, authority to bless. These blessings are the opposite of the curses and the hatred which drove them.

19. Ancestors, father, imams, Muslim leaders, and any others who influenced me to curse myself.

20. He thought his apartment might be under a curse.

21. He didn't know how to break a curse.

22. He needed to take authority in the name of Jesus to break all curses against his home.

23. They are experiencing curses.

24. Nine steps: 1) Confess and repent. 2) Remove ungodly objects. 3) Forgive others and yourself. 4) Claim your authority in Christ. 5) Renounce and break the curse. 6) Declare your freedom in Christ. 7) Command demons to leave (casting them out). 8) Declare blessings. 9) Praise God.

Lesson 8 answers

1. Four reasons: 1) Pain of loss of community. 2) Obstacles and roadblocks from Islam. 3) Direct persecution. 4) Disappointment with Christians and church.

2. Churches turn away converts from Islam because of fear and the *dhimma* rules.

3. Understand and reject the *dhimma* covenant.

4. Fear, a sense of insecurity and love of money, feelings of rejection, a sense of victimhood, taking offense, inability to trust others, emotional pain, sexual sin, gossip, and lying.

5. The controlling influence of Islam.

6. Others will be jealous.

7. He took offense at other Christians.

8. The churches compete with each church believing it is better than others.

9. A door left open and the house left empty.

10. Healthy Christians.

11. Habits and ways of thinking need to change.

12. Paul wants to encourage Titus to keep growing.

13. Paul used to hate Christians.

14. By growing in love, knowledge, and depth of insight, and bearing good fruit.

15. [Participants report negative effects they have observed.]

16. He renounced and broke a generational curse. He was also healed of a tendency to suffer anxiety.

17. Close *all* the doors.

18. Close open doors which Satan can use against the believer.

19. The soul is meant to contain the water of life, but if there are gaps in its side, it cannot hold as much water as it should.

20. Similar obstacles and soul damage for BMBs seeking to live for Christ.

21. It helps them feel superior.

22. Churches have trouble working together. People can be jealous when others advance in ministry. People do not want to serve as leaders because they think they will be attacked.

23. Six teachings: 1) Valuing the heart of a servant. 2) Finding your identity in Christ, not in what you say or do or what others say or think about you. 3) Learning to boast in your weaknesses. 4) Learning to rejoice in others' successes, and grieve with them when they are suffering. 5) Learning how to speak the truth in love. 6) Learning about the destructive effects of gossip.

24. People cannot grow because they hide their problems and do not want help with them.

25. Six topics: 1) Forgiveness. 2) Rejection and offense. 3) Building trust. 4) Renouncing witchcraft. 5) Women and men respecting each other and speaking the truth to each other. 6) Parents blessing their children instead of cursing them.

26. So people can rebuild their whole worldview.

27. Steve made converts quickly but couldn't keep them. Cheri made converts slowly but they kept on with Christ. Cheri's approach worked better because when people decided to follow Jesus they understood well what they were committing to.

28. Six steps: 1) Two confessions. 2) Turning away. 3) Requests. 4) Transfer allegiance. 5) Promise and consecration. 6) Declaration.

29. Steps 4-6.

30. Satan.

31. Renounce Islam by praying the 'Declaration and Prayer to Renounce the *Shahada* and Break Its Power'.

32. More mature BMB pastors.

33. To make sure you have the best person, and to help them be ready for leadership.

34. They don't learn humility, and they may experience rejection from others.

35. Regularly: at least once a week.

36. Applying the Bible to practical daily challenges. This helps their character to grow to be more like Christ's.

37. To model transparency to the trainee.

38. To avoid shame.

39. So they can learn to deal with challenging issues.

40. If bondages are not removed and wounds healed, this will limit a person's fruitfulness in ministry. Also, if someone is set free they know better how to help others become free.

41. So they can endure in ministry, and be trusted.

42. Servant-hearted mutual love and respect.

43. So we can receive critical feedback and grow in maturity.

44. To model self-awareness to the trainee.

45. Because they cannot avoid it.

46. To honor God, receive God's blessing for the church, and learn humility.

Made in the USA
Monee, IL
25 August 2023

41645540R00154